Dress Your Cookie

Bake Them!　　Dress Them!　　Eat Them!

Dress Your **Cookie**

Bake Them!   Dress Them!   Eat Them!

Joanna Farrow

spruce

An Hachette UK Company
www.hachette.co.uk

First published in Great Britain in 2012 by Spruce
a division of Octopus Publishing Group Ltd
Endeavour House, 189 Shaftesbury Avenue,
London WC2H 8JY
www.octopusbooks.co.uk
www.octopusbooks.usa.com

Distributed in the US by
Hachette Book Group USA
237 Park Avenue, New York, NY 10017 USA

Distributed in Canada by
Canadian Manda Group
165 Dufferin Street, Toronto, Ontario, Canada M6K 3H6

Copyright © Octopus Publishing Group Ltd 2012

Publisher: Sarah Ford
Editor: Camilla Davis
Cover design and book development: Eoghan O'Brien
Designer: Michelle Tilly
Photography: Lis Parsons
Food styling: Joanna Farrow
Production: Caroline Alberti

ISBN 978-1-84601-392-8

Printed and bound in China

10 9 8 7 6 5 4 3 2 1

This book includes dishes made with nuts and nut
derivatives. It is advisable for those with known allergic
reactions to nuts and nut derivatives and those who
may be potentially vulnerable to these allergies, such
as pregnant and nursing mothers, invalids, the elderly,
babies, and children, to avoid dishes made with nuts
and nut oils. It is also prudent to check the labels of
prepared ingredients for the possible inclusion of nut
derivatives. Some icings include raw eggs. It is prudent
for the potentially vulnerable (as before) to avoid raw
or lightly cooked eggs. Small candies are suggested as
decoration. Care should be taken if used by or served to
small children.

Glossary

- All-purpose flour = plain flour
- Candy-coated chocolates = M&Ms, Smarties, etc.
- Chewy fruit rolls = fruit leathers and winders
- Plastic wrap = cling film
- Confectioners' sugar = icing sugar
- Corn syrup = golden syrup
- Decorator frosting = writing icing
- Decorating sugar = sanding sugar
- Decorating dust = dusting powder
- Dragées = sugar balls
- Fondant sugar = fondant icing sugar
- Glucose syrup = liquid glucose
- Gummy candies = gums, gumdrops, wine gums, etc.
- Hard candies = boiled sweets
- Licorice laces = liquorice whips
- Decorating tip = nozzle
- Semisweet chocolate = plain chocolate
- Superfine sugar = caster sugar

Contents

Making Cookies	6	Pumpkin Pie	68
Shaping Cookies Before Baking	8	Trick or Treat Bucket	70
Making Buttercream and Other Icings	10	Haunted House	72
Decorating Techniques using Rolled Fondant	12	Christmas Bauble	74
Melting and Using Chocolate	16	Christmas Star	76
Piping Techniques	18	Christmas Tree	78
Decorating with Candies	20	Snowman	80
Useful Equipment	22	Hot Dog	82
Pirate	24	Popcorn	84
Racing Car Driver	26	Teapot	86
Pierrot Lunaire	28	Wedding Cake	88
Funny Face	30	Ice Cream Cone	90
Curled Flamingo	32	Strawberry	92
Peacock	34	Gingerbread House	94
Westie Dog	36	Teddy Bear	96
Festival Elephant	38	Princess' Crown	98
Fish	40	Kiddie's Car	100
Chubby Owl	42	Spaceship	102
Dragonfly	44	Eyeball	104
Trophy	46	Sun	106
Paint Palette	48	Bikini	108
Topiary Tree	50	Designer Shopping Bag	110
Ace of Hearts	52	Platform Shoes	112
Trainers	54	Vintage Dress	114
Pink Heart	56	Mask	116
Easter Basket	58	Art Attack	118
Birthday Cake	60	Ammonite Fossil	120
Baby Booties	62		
Mortarboard	64	Templates	122
Bollywood	66	Source List	128

Making Cookies

Cookies can be baked in almost any shape, providing a perfect blank canvas for decorating in a feast of fabulous ways. From simple buttercream toppings to artistic and intricate designs, there are cookie designs in this book for everyone, regardless of creative skills. The basic cookie recipe is easy to mix and bake, leaving you plenty of time to make your required icings and to gather a selection of candies with which to decorate your cookies.

Ingredients

- 1¹/₄ cups (150 g) all-purpose flour
- 7 tablespoons (100 g) lightly salted firm butter, diced
- ¹/₃ cup (50 g) confectioners' sugar
- 1 egg yolk
- 1 teaspoon vanilla extract or bean paste

Vanilla cookies

This dough recipe generally makes enough for six cookies, depending on the cookie size. However, you might be able to squeeze out one or two more cookies from the dough by rerolling the trimmings. The quantity can easily be doubled to make a larger batch.

Making the dough

1. Put the flour and butter in a food processor and blend until the mixture resembles fine breadcrumbs. Briefly blend in the sugar.

2. Add the egg yolk and vanilla and blend again until the mixture comes together to make a smooth dough. (Alternatively you can rub the butter into the flour in a bowl, then add the remaining ingredients and knead into a dough).

3. Turn the dough out onto a lightly floured surface and knead gently to incorporate any stray crumbs. Wrap in plastic wrap and chill for at least 1 hour before rolling.

Baking the dough

1.

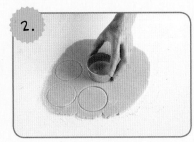

2.

Roll out the cookie dough on a lightly floured surface until about $1/4$ inch (5 mm) thick. If the dough is too firm to roll, leave it to stand at room temperature for 20–30 minutes. The firmer the dough when you roll it, the less likely it will lose its shape during baking.

Cut out shapes using a cutter, ruler or template as required in the chosen recipe. Dusting the cookie cutter or knife with flour will help make a clean, non-sticky cut. (The dough can then be gathered up, lightly kneaded and rerolled to make extra shapes).

Flavor variations

Ginger cookies Replace the confectioners' sugar with light brown sugar and add 1 teaspoon ground ginger instead of the vanilla.
Chocolate cookies Replace scant $1/4$ cup (25 g) of the flour with $1/4$ cup (25 g) unsweetened cocoa powder.
Lemon cookies Add the finely grated zest of 1 lemon and replace the vanilla with 1 teaspoon of lemon juice.

3.

4.

Place the shapes on a lightly greased cookie sheet, spacing them slightly apart to allow for spreading. Bake in a preheated oven, 375°F (190°C, Gas 5), for 12–15 minutes. The paler cookies doughs will be done when they start turning golden around the edges. Chocolate cookies will look baked, but will not darken much.

Remove the cookies from the oven and leave the shapes on the cookie sheet for 2 minutes before transferring to a cooling rack (or 5 minutes for shapes that you've molded together— see page 8). The high sugar content of the cookies means they will be slightly soft when they come out of the oven and will crisp up as they cool.

Shaping Cookies Before Baking

Some of the cookies are baked in more intricate shapes using a template made from parchment paper (see below) or by molding different shapes together such as the trophy on page 46. Have any templates ready before you roll out the dough.

Using a template

Cut out the required template. Roll out the dough, then, starting at one edge of the dough, place the template on the dough. Dip the blade of a small, sharp knife in flour and then cut cleanly around the template. Transfer the cookie shape to a lightly greased cookie sheet, gently easing the dough back together if it has torn. Cut out the remaining shapes and bake as described in the cookie recipe. Use a craft knife for more intricate shapes, and work on a floured chopping board so the work surface does not get scratched.

Molding cookie shapes

You can have a lot of fun creating your own cookies by cutting out different shapes and pressing them together before baking. Have beaten egg white and a paintbrush ready to use as "glue".

Cut out the required shapes from the dough, either using cookie cutters or a knife. Brush a little egg white over the edges of dough to be joined, then place the edges next to each other and use your fingers to push the pieces together. Transfer the shapes to a lightly greased cookie sheet and bake as described in the cookie recipe.

Adding candies when baking

Effects, such as "windows", can look stunning and are easily created by baking crushed hard candies in cut out sections of the cookie dough.

1. Line the cookie sheet with parchment paper. This is essential or the candies will stick on the cookie sheet. Roll and shape the dough as required, then cut out the chosen shapes from the dough. Place the cookie shape on the lined cookie sheet and bake in a preheated oven at 375°F (190°C, Gas 5) for 5 minutes.

2. Meanwhile, with the candies still in their wrappers, crush them using a rolling pin. Remove the cookies from the oven and place a few pieces of crushed candy in the cut out sections of the dough. A small section such as a little heart shaped window (see page 95) will require a pea-sized piece of candy; a large area, such as the Christmas star centers (see page 77) will need a whole crushed candy.

3. Return the cookies to the oven and bake for a further 6–7 minutes until the cookies are baked and the candies have melted and spread to fill the space. Remove from the oven, leave on the cookie sheet for 5–10 minutes, or until the candies have turned brittle, then peel away the paper and transfer the cookies to a cooling rack to cool completely.

Creating holes in cookies

Baked cookies can be threaded with ribbon as an additional decoration, such as the handles of the Designer Shopping Bag on page 111, or for hanging up decorations.

1. Roll and shape the dough as required, then place on a lightly greased baking sheet. Push the handle end of a fine paintbrush or a metal skewer into the cookie dough and rotate it slightly to make a hole about $1/4$ inch (5 mm) in diameter. Bake as described in the cookie recipe.

2. Immediately after baking while the dough is still soft, remake the holes by pushing the handle end of the paintbrush or metal skewer into the previously made holes and carefully rotating as before. The dough will have expanded slightly during baking and the holes might have closed up.

Making Buttercream and Other Icings

These basic recipes are used repeatedly throughout the book. Rolled fondant is easy to make at home, though you may find it simpler to buy ready-to-use rolled fondant, which comes in white and a wide range of other colors.

Flavor variations

Chocolate buttercream
Replace $^1/_2$ oz (15 g) of the confectioners' sugar with $^1/_2$ oz (15 g) unsweetened cocoa powder.

Lemon buttercream Add 2 teaspoons lemon juice instead of the vanilla.

Vanilla buttercream

This is used for more basic decorating techniques, such as spreading or piping, and as a base before adding layers of rolled fondant. It's easy to color and flavor, and keeps well in the refrigerator for several days. Simply soften and beat with a wooden spoon so that it's creamy again, before using. The quantities can easily be doubled if the recipe requires.

Ingredients

- 3 tablespoons (40 g) unsalted butter, softened
- Scant $^1/_2$ cup (65 g) confectioners' sugar
- $^1/_2$ teaspoon vanilla extract

1. Put the butter, sugar, and vanilla extract in a bowl and beat well with a hand-held electric beater until light and fluffy. If you are not using the buttercream immediately, cover the surface with plastic wrap to stop a crust forming.

Ingredients

- 1 egg white
- 1^1/$_2$ cups (200 g) confectioners' sugar

Royal icing

Royal icing sugar is available from most supermarkets and is easy to make up by adding water, as directed on the packet. Homemade royal icing is also very convenient, but make sure you use good quality egg whites. Both will keep well in the fridge for several days, provided the surface is tightly covered with plastic wrap. If the recipe requires small amounts of piped icing, tubes of decorator frosting make a good substitute, and come in various colors. Royal icing is also used for "flooding" cookie decorations with icing. This technique requires a softer consistency (see page 19).

1. Put the egg white in a bowl and beat lightly to break it up. Add half the sugar and beat until smooth.

2. Gradually work in the remaining sugar until the icing has a soft, smooth consistency that just holds its shape.

Ingredients

- 1 egg white
- 2 tablespoons glucose syrup or light corn syrup
- About 3^1/$_2$ cups (500 g) confectioners' sugar

Homemade rolled fondant

Fondant is used frequently in this book, as it's so easy to roll and cut out or mold into any shape. Additionally, white rolled fondant is easily colored by kneading in food coloring and keeps well as long as it's tightly covered in plastic wrap to prevent a crust forming. See pages 12–15 for instructions on how to use rolled fondant.

1. Put the egg white, glucose syrup or light corn syrup, and about one-quarter of the sugar in a bowl and mix to a smooth paste.

2. Continue to mix in more sugar until it becomes too stiff to stir. Turn the paste out onto the work surface and knead in more sugar to make a smooth, stiff paste. (If the fondant is too soft and sticky it will be difficult to work with.)

3. Wrap the fondant tightly in several thicknesses of plastic wrap to prevent a crust forming and the texture spoiling—unless you're going to be using it immediately.

Decorating Techniques Using Rolled Fondant

The following pages explain various techniques that are used frequently in the recipes and will transform your cookies into something very special, from creating uniquely shaped cookies using templates to using colored rolled fondant to make different shapes and features. All the techniques are easy to master, even for first-time decorators.

Making and using templates

Besides templates for actual cookie shapes, this book provides templates for decorating the cookies using rolled fondant. Trace the shape onto parchment paper, or other lightweight paper then, using a pair of scissors, cut out the shape. Thinly roll out the rolled fondant on a surface dusted with confectioners' sugar. (Some of the recipes also use thinly rolled chewy candies for cutting around). Rest the template on top of the rolled fondant or candy and carefully cut around it using the tip of a small, sharp knife or craft knife. If using a craft knife, work on a chopping board so as not to mark the work surface.

Using rolled fondant

Great fun to use, this icing is soft and pliable, and can be molded or rolled out and cut into any shape. Use a little confectioners' sugar to dust the work surface, or your fingers if molding shapes, before you start. This will stop the fondant sticking to the surface or your hands, particularly on a warm day. Any fondant that's not being worked with should be wrapped in plastic wrap, as it quickly dries out and its texture will be spoiled. If the surface of the fondant dries out because it hasn't been completely sealed, cut off and discard the edges—the center should still be soft and pliable.

Rolling shapes into rolled fondant

Adding rolled fondant shapes to a rolled fondant in a contrasting color makes an easy and effective decoration. The spotty effect shown here is used to create the pirate's headscarf on page 25. Use exactly the same technique for impressing other shapes such as cut out hearts or stripes. You'll need to work reasonably quickly with this technique so the icings don't dry out before you've finished.

I. Thinly roll out some rolled fondant on a surface lightly dusted with confectioners' sugar. Break off tiny pieces of fondant in a contrasting color, roll into balls and space then about $^3/_4$ inch (2 cm) apart all over the fondant.

2. Dust a rolling pin very lightly with confectioners' sugar and roll it two or three times over the fondant, lifting the fondant after each roll so it doesn't stick to the surface. Cut out shapes as required.

Adding color

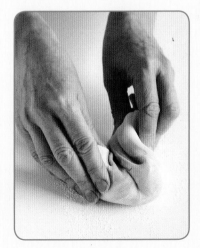

Rolled fondant is available in white and basic colors from supermarkets, or in a wider range of colors from specialty cake decorating stores or online suppliers. In many of the recipes you only need a small amount of certain colors, so it makes good sense to color your own. Liquid food colorings are generally acceptable for a pastel shade, but for stronger colors, paste food colorings are more effective. Working on a surface lightly dusted with confectioners' sugar, dot the color onto the fondant with a toothpick and knead it in. Use the food coloring sparingly at first, until you're sure of the strength of the coloring—you can always blend in more to give a more vibrant shade.

Shaping frills

To create a delicate "frilly" edge, dust a toothpick lightly with confectioners' sugar and run it horizontally along the edge of the piece of fondant so the fondant starts to ruffle. Lift the fondant from the surface and redust so the ruffle doesn't stick, then roll the fondant with the toothpick again. (The more you roll the toothpick over the fondant, the more ruffled the edge will become). Trim off the unruffled edge of the strip if it's become uneven, then carefully lift the ruffle from the surface and secure in place. Once positioned, the ruffles can be lifted and folded with the tip of a toothpick.

Blending colors

Basic primary colors can be kneaded together to create more unusual colors. Use the same principle as mixing paints. Red and yellow can be mixed to make orange; blue and red to make purple; red and white to make pink; and black and white to make grey.

Securing shapes in place

Where rolled fondant is laid onto a cookie, the surface should first be spread with a little melted chocolate or buttercream to serve as "glue". Don't spread it too thickly or the rolled fondant won't be as easy to arrange in place. Where rolled fondant is secured to another layer of fondant, it's best to very lightly brush the fondant with a dampened paintbrush. Dip the paintbrush in a dish of cold water and brush it against the side of the dish to remove the excess water. If too much water is left on the brush, the fondant won't stay neatly in place and the texture of the fondant will be spoilt.

Shaping plunger cutter flowers

Plunger cutters are fun to use and look so professional and effective. Roll out the rolled fondant as thinly as you can on a surface lightly dusted with confectioners' sugar, ideally about $1/16$ inch (1.5 mm) thick. Cut out the flower shape with the cutter. Position the cutter on the cookie where you want the flower decoration and push it out with the plunger. If securing to a dried fondant, you'll probably need to lightly moisten it with a dampened paintbrush so the flower sticks in place (see above).

Melting and Using Chocolate

Melted chocolate can be used for piping simple or more intricate shapes and for spooning directly onto the cookies. Avoid overheating or you'll spoil its smooth texture.

To melt on the stove Chop the chocolate into small pieces and put in a heatproof bowl. Set the bowl over a saucepan of gently simmering water, making sure the base of the bowl doesn't come in contact with the water. Once the chocolate starts to melt, turn off the heat and leave until completely melted, stirring once or twice until no lumps remain.

To melt in a microwave Chop the chocolate into small pieces and put in a microwave-proof bowl. Melt in 1-minute spurts, checking frequently until the chocolate is partially melted. Remove the bowl and stir until the remaining chocolate has melted in its own heat. Take care when melting white chocolate as the high sugar content makes it more likely to burn in the microwave.

Using chocolate for piping

Melted chocolate can also be used for piping lines or dots (see page 19). It is best done without fitting a decorating tip into the pastry bag, as chocolate sets quite quickly in the bag. If the chocolate does set, you can soften it by popping the bag very briefly in the microwave, but this cannot be done if a metal decorating tip is used.

Making a paper pastry bag

Paper pastry bags are easy to make and are great for piping melted chocolate, royal icing, or buttercream. Both parchment and waxed paper can be used. For filling and using pastry bags, see pages 18–19.

1.

Cut out a 10-inch (25-cm) square of parchment paper. Fold it diagonally in half and then cut the paper in half, just to one side of the fold. Take one triangle and hold it with the long edge facing away from you while holding the point nearest you with one hand.

2.

Curl the right-hand point over to meet the center point, shaping a cone.

3.

Bring the left-hand point over the cone so the three points meet.

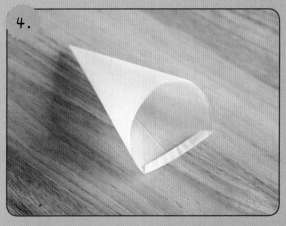

4.

Fold the points over several times so the cone shape is secured in place.

Piping Techniques

Piping is a skill that is so easily mastered with a little practice, and the results are so rewarding. A decorating tip is not absolutely necessary for simple lines, dots, or outlines. It does, however, give a cleaner, more precise shape that ultimately looks more professional. For shaping stars a star decorating tip is essential. Buttercream and royal icing are both suitable for piping decorations.

Filling a paper pastry bag fitted with a decorating tip
1. Cut off the end about $^3/_4$ inch (2 cm) from the point of the bag, and insert the decorating tip in the pastry bag.

2. Half fill the pastry bag with buttercream or icing and twist the open end together to secure. Keep this end twisted firmly together.

Filling a paper pastry bag without a decorating tip Use the same technique as above, but don't cut off the tip of the bag before filling. Once filled and the pastry bag end is twisted to seal, snip off the tip. Some of the recipes require the merest amount to be snipped off the end of the bag, so the icing can be piped in a thin line. This is particularly important if you're piping an outline or fine detail. You can always snip off more of the tip if the line is too thin.

Piping stars
Fit the bag with a small star decorating tip. Hold the bag almost vertically over the cookie and squeeze out a small amount of icing until the star is the size you want. Release the pressure and move the bag away crisply to give a neat shape.

Piping lines, dots, and beading

For piped lines, squeeze the pastry bag gently, keeping the pastry bag raised slightly above the cookie and work at a speed that suits you. For straight lines, hold the pastry bag at about 45° and keep a constant pressure as you squeeze out the icing. For dots, hold the bag more vertically and squeeze tiny amounts of icing out, releasing the pressure before you lift the bag away. For decorative beading, hold the bag at about 45°, squeeze out a dot of icing, release the pressure, move the bag fractionally backward and squeeze another dot. Repeat, as required. You'll start to work much faster with a little practice.

Flooding shapes

To create shapes to decorate cookies, an outline is piped in royal icing. This outline is then "flooded" with a slightly thinner consistency of royal icing (see page 11) or chocolate. Flooding gives a smooth and professional looking finish to which you can add further decorations.

1.	2.	3.

To pipe the outline, first color the royal icing, if the recipe requires, then put the icing in a paper pastry bag fitted with a fine plain decorator tip, see page 18. Pipe lines or curves slightly in from the edge of the cookie, following the outline of the area that is to be filled with icing. Alternatively use a tube of decorator frosting.

Put a little more royal icing in a small bowl, adding liquid or paste food coloring, if necessary, then stir in a few drops of cold water so that the icing becomes smooth and the surface levels a few seconds after you stop stirring. Take care not to add too much water, as the icing will quickly become too thin to manage.

Put the thinned icing in a separate paper pastry bag and cut off a small tip. Pipe into the area, spreading the icing into the corners with a toothpick. For a perfect finish, ideally the icing should be left to set for a few hours or overnight before adding further decorations, but they can be added straight away if it's more convenient.

Decorating with Candies

Soft chewy candies make great decorations, as they are pliable and can be molded easily. They're great fun to use, but will slowly soften and eventually lose their shape so, if using chewy candies, don't decorate your cookies more than a day in advance. The softness of a candy depends on the brand used and the ambient temperature. If you can squeeze it between your thumb and forefinger, it can probably be shaped without heating. If it's firm or brittle, you may have to heat it in the microwave first.

Softening candies

Place the required amount of chewy candy on a piece of parchment paper and heat on full power in the microwave for a few seconds. The softening time will depend on the temperature, the amount of sugar in the sweet, and how many chews you're microwaving at one time. Time the softening of the candies very cautiously. Some might take a few seconds and others more like 20 seconds. If left for too long, you might end up with a puddle of boiling syrup on the microwave base so be careful.

Molding candies

Once softened and pliable, you can mold the candy or a piece of the candy into the required shape just as you would mold rolled fondant. Position the shape on the cookie and secure it with a dot of frosting when necessary.

Flattening candies

Soften the candies as above if brittle and then flatten with a rolling pin. Continue rolling until it is the desired thickness. Soft licorice can also be flattened in this way though you won't need to heat it first.

Using other candies for decorating

Many of the designs use small candies for adding finishing touches. Most candies, particularly soft fruit chews and gummy candies, can be cut into small pieces so they look more effective. Flat gummy candies and chewy fruit rolls can also be cut with scissors or cut out using a template.

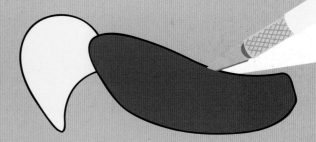

Making colored sugar sprinkles

Coloring your own sugar makes a useful alternative to store-bought "decorating" or "sanding" sugar, as you can create any color you want using paste food colorings. Put superfine or granulated sugar in a small bowl and add a dot of food coloring paste. Using the back of a teaspoon, "mash" the coloring against the side of the bowl so it starts to color the sugar. Continue to work the color into the sugar until evenly blended, adding more color if you prefer a darker shade.

Useful Equipment

Making and decorating cookies requires minimal equipment. Here are a few tools that will help making your cookie creations easier and also more professional looking. You'll probably already own many of them.

Cookie cutters

The cookie cutters used in this book are round, heart, star, or flower shaped. Any other shapes are made by using a template or shaping with a knife. There is a wide range of cookie cutters available to buy, many of them seasonal, so you can stock up on them to increase your repertoire. The most useful cutters to have for making the cookies in this book are a set of round ones that range from $^3/_4$ inch (2 cm) to $3^1/_2$ inches (8.5 cm) in diameter.

Small sharp knife

A small cook's knife is useful for cutting out small shapes in rolled fondant and for cutting candies into smaller pieces.

Craft knife

The sharp, fine-edged tip of this tool is useful for cutting out small, intricate shapes from rolled fondant, where a larger knife might be less precise, and for cutting shapes from candies. Always work on a chopping board when using, as the sharp point can easily damage a work surface. A small cook's knife can be used instead.

Freezer bags

A small plastic freezer bag makes a useful, shortcut improvisation for a pastry bag. Spoon the buttercream or icing into one corner of the bag and twist the bag so the icing is pushed right into the corner with no air spaces. Cut off the merest tip for piping. This is particularly useful when flooding shapes with thinned royal icing.

Decorating cutters

Small decorative cutters, such as flower, star, and heart shapes, are used for some of the rolled fondant decorations. These are worth buying if you intend to make lots of cookies, but many shapes can be made using a knife or by using your own templates. When making tiny flower shapes, flower plunger cutters are particularly useful, as you can press them out so easily and quickly position them directly onto cookie.

Rolling pin

A regular pastry rolling pin is fine for rolling out the cookie dough, but for rolling out small pieces of rolled fondant and chewy candies a smaller rolling pin is easier to manage. Those included in kids baking kits are ideal, or use a cake decorator's rolling pin, available from specialty stores.

Toothpicks

These are useful for dotting paste food coloring from its pot onto buttercream, royal icing, and rolled fondant before kneading in. They're also used for easing royal icing into corners when spreading the icing over cookies. Small metal skewers can be used instead.

Paintbrushes

Fine tipped paintbrushes are ideal for painting food coloring onto icing. They're also used in many of the recipes that use rolled fondant, for securing decorations in place.

Pastry bags

The recipes in this book are designed for using small paper pastry bags. These are disposable, easy to make (see Making a pastry bag, page 17) and don't necessarily need a decorating tip (see chosen recipe). Paper bags can also be bought ready made from cookware and cake decorating stores. Washable bags, which are reusable, are also available but must be fitted with a decorating tip to use.

Metal spatula

A small, flexible spatula is useful for spreading buttercream, royal icing, or chocolate over a cookie when you want a fairly smooth surface for adding decorations.

Decorating tips

These enable you to pipe different shapes onto cookies. They're available in many different designs, although the only ones required for this book are a fine plain tip for writing and "star", and "leaf" tips (see page 50).

Pirate

Ingredients

- 1 quantity ginger cookie dough (see page 7)
- Flour, for dusting
- 1 egg white, beaten
- 3^1/$_2$ oz (100 g) blue rolled fondant
- Confectioners' sugar, for dusting
- 1^1/$_2$ oz (40 g) red rolled fondant
- 8 pieces soft black licorice
- Tube of black decorator frosting
- 1 oz (25 g) white rolled fondant
- 6 blue candy-coated chocolates
- 6 red flat round candies, such as Lifesavers

Equipment

- Large cookie sheet
- Rolling pin
- 3^1/$_2$-inch (8.5-cm) round cookie cutter
- ^{3}/$_4$-inch (2-cm) round cookie cutter
- 1^1/$_2$-inch (3.5-cm) cookie cutter
- Fine paintbrush
- Parchment paper, for tracing
- Pencil
- Scissors
- Craft knife

Baking: Heat the oven to 375°F (190°C, Gas 6) and grease a large cookie sheet. Roll out the dough on a lightly floured surface until about ^{1}/$_4$ inch (5 mm) thick and cut out 6 cookies using a 3^1/$_2$-inch (8.5-cm) round cookie cutter. Place the dough rounds on the cookie sheet, spacing them well apart. Gather up the trimmings and reroll the dough. Cut out 6 rounds using a ^{3}/$_4$-inch (2-cm) round cookie cutter, then cut the rounds in half. (Alternatively, roll small balls of the dough, press flat until about ^{1}/$_4$ inch (5 mm) thick and cut in half). Brush a little egg white, using a fine paintbrush, over the cut edges of dough halves and position the halves on either side of each of the large dough rounds for ears. Gently press together to secure. Bake in the preheated oven for 12–15 minutes until lightly browned around the edges. Remove from the oven, leave on the cookie sheet for 5 minutes, then transfer to a cooling rack to cool completely.

Head scarves: Trace and cut out the template for the Pirate's headscarf (opposite). Roll out the blue rolled fondant on a surface dusted with confectioners' sugar until about ^{1}/$_{16}$ inch (2 mm) thick and use the red rolled fondant to make a spotty effect (see page 13.) Keep aside enough red fondant to make the noses. Place the template on the spotted fondant and cut around. Repeat to give 6 headscarves. Secure in place with black decorator frosting.

Eye patches: Flatten the licorice pieces with a rolling pin until about ^{1}/$_8$ inch (2.5 mm) thick. Cut out 6 semi-circular shapes using an 1^1/$_2$-inch (3.5-cm) cookie cutter and secure 1 shape on each cookie in place, as in the picture, with black decorator frosting. Cut 6 long thin strips of licorice and secure above the eye patch, trimming off the ends to the correct length.

Faces: Roll 6 tiny balls of red fondant between your finger and thumb and secure in place for noses. Roll 6 slightly larger balls of the white fondant and press flat until about $^1/_4$ inch (5 mm) thick. Secure in place for eyes, then secure a blue candy-coated chocolate on top of each eye. Pipe on each cookie a wonky, smiling mouth with the black decorator frosting and add plenty of dots for stubble. Roll out some white fondant and cut out 18 squares for teeth as small as you can shape them. Press 3 squares into the black frosting on each cookie. Use a little more decorator frosting to secure the flat round candies for earrings.

Shiver me cookies

Ahoy there matey!

Look at my candy earring

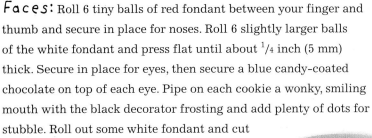

Racing Car Driver

Ingredients

- 1 quantity ginger cookie dough (see page 7)
- Flour, for dusting
- 1 quantity royal icing (see page 11)
- Lemon juice, for thinning
- Small piece white rolled fondant
- Tubes of red and black decorator frosting
- Brown, black, and blue food colorings
- 1 short length of sugar-coated red chewy fruit roll
- Chocolate or colored star sprinkles

Equipment

- Large cookie sheet
- Rolling pin
- Small sharp knife
- 3-inch (7.5-cm) round cookie cutter
- 2 paper pastry bags (see page 17)
- Fine round decorating tip
- Toothpick
- Fine paintbrush

Baking: Heat the oven to 375°F (190°C, Gas 6) and grease a large cookie sheet. Roll out the dough on a lightly floured surface until about $1/4$ inch (5 mm) thick and cut out 6 cookies using a 3-inch (7.5-cm) round cookie cutter. Slice one side off each cookie to create a basic helmet shape. Place the dough rounds on the cookie sheet, spacing them slightly apart. Gather up the trimmings and reroll to make extra cookies, if liked. Bake in the preheated oven for 12–15 minutes until lightly browned around the edges. Remove from the oven, leave on the cookie sheet for 2 minutes, and then transfer to a cooling rack to cool completely.

Helmets: Put 1–2 tablespoons of royal icing in a paper pastry bag fitted with a fine round decorating tip. Use to pipe outlines around the edges of the helmet shapes, leaving a slight edge. Pipe a rectangular "window", measuring about $2 \times 1^{1}/4$ inches (5 x 3 cm), near the straight edge of the icing on each cookie for the face area. Add a few drops of lemon juice to the remaining icing to give a thinner consistency (see page 19). Put the icing in a second paper pastry bag and snip $1/4$ inch (5 mm) off the tip. Pipe the icing inside the outlined helmet areas, spreading it out with a toothpick. Leave to set for several hours or overnight.

Faces and hair: Roll tiny balls of white rolled fondant between your finger and thumb and secure in place with decorator frosting for eyes. Pipe noses and mouths onto each cookie using red decorator frosting, and pipe the hair using black decorator frosting. Use a fine paintbrush to pipe the centers of the eyes with brown food coloring.

Zoom! ZOOM! Zoom! ZOOOOMM!

Finishing touches: Use black food coloring to paint a chequered strip down the center of each helmet. Cut out thin strips of chewy fruit candy and position on the helmets with a dampened paintbrush, if necessary, as in the picture. Secure 3 star sprinkles on each helmet. Using a fine paintbrush and blue food coloring, add further detail to each helmet.

Go faster stripes

Eat me before I race off

Pierrot Lunaire

Ingredients

- 1 quantity lemon cookie dough (see page 7)
- Flour, for dusting
- 1 quantity royal icing (see page 11)
- A little lemon juice, for thinning
- 3½ oz (100 g) black rolled fondant
- Confectioners' sugar, for dusting
- 7 oz (200 g) white rolled fondant
- Black food coloring
- 1 oz (25 g) red rolled fondant

Equipment

- Large cookie sheet
- Rolling pin
- 3-inch and 1½-inch (7.5 cm and 4 cm) round cookie cutters
- Paper pastry bag (see page 17)
- Parchment paper, for tracing
- Pencil
- Scissors
- Craft knife
- Fine paintbrush
- Toothpick

Baking: Heat the oven to 375°F (190°C, Gas 6) and grease a large cookie sheet. Roll out the dough on a lightly floured surface until about ¼ inch (5 mm) thick and cut out 6 cookies using a 3-inch (7.5-cm) round cookie cutter. Use the rolling pin to stretch one half of each round so it becomes slightly egg shaped. Place the dough shapes on the cookie sheet, spacing them slightly apart. Reroll the trimmings to make extra cookies, if liked. Bake in the preheated oven for 12–15 minutes until lightly browned around the edges. Leave on the cookie sheet for 2 minutes then transfer to a cooling rack to cool completely.

White faces: Put a little of the royal icing in a paper pastry bag and snip off the merest tip. Use to pipe outlines around the edges of the cookies. Stir a few drops of lemon juice into the remaining icing to give a thinner consistency (see page 19). Spoon the soft royal icing into the outline areas, spreading the icing into a thin layer with the back of a teaspoon. Leave to set for several hours or overnight.

Head Scarves: Trace and cut out the template for Pierrot's head scarf (opposite). Roll out the black rolled fondant on a surface dusted with confectioners' sugar until about 1/16 inch (2 mm). Place the template on the fondant and cut around the template. Repeat to give 6 head scarves. Moisten the tops of the heads with a dampened paintbrush and press the fondant gently in place.

Faces: Trace and cut out the templates for Pierrot's eyes and mouth (opposite). Roll out a little of the white fondant and cut out 6 sets of eyes. Press one set of eyes onto each cookie, securing in place with a dampened paintbrush if necessary. Roll out the black fondant trimmings, then cut out the 6 mouths and secure in place.

Dilute a little black food coloring with water and use to paint the eyes, eyebrows, noses, and tiny teardrops on each cookie, as in the picture.

Frilly collars: Roll out the remaining white fondant until about $^1/_{16}$ inch (2 mm) thick and cut out six 3-inch (7.5 cm) rounds using a cookie cutter. Cut out the centers using an $1^1/_2$-inch (4-cm) cookie cutter, then cut the rings in half. Roll a toothpick around the outer edges of each semicircle so that it starts to frill (see page 14). Pipe a line of white royal icing around the chin area of the cookies and secure one semicircle of frill onto each of the piped lines. Pipe a further line of icing on the straight edge of the frill and secure a second layer of frill. Using the tip of a toothpick, lift up the frilled edges to open them out.

Flowers: Take a pea-sized ball of red fondant and roll it under your fingers until about $2^1/_2$ inches (6 cm) long. Flatten into a long strip with a rolling pin, then roll the strip up to resemble a simple flower shape. Secure in place with a dot of royal icing. Repeat for the remaining cookies.

Funny Face

Ingredients

- 1 quantity lemon cookie dough (see page 7)
- Flour, for dusting
- Tubes of white, red, and green decorator frosting
- 12 mini candy-coated chocolates
- Yellow food coloring
- 1 quantity lemon buttercream (see page 10)

Equipment

- Large cookie sheet
- Rolling pin
- 3-inch (7.5-cm) round cookie cutter
- Paper pastry bag (see page 17)
- Scissors

Baking: Heat the oven to 375°F (190°C, Gas 6) and grease a large cookie sheet. Roll out the dough on a lightly floured surface until about $1/4$ inch (5 mm) thick and cut out 6 cookies using a 3-inch (7.5-cm) round cookie cutter. Place the dough rounds on the cookie sheet, spacing them well apart. Gather up the trimmings and reroll to make extra cookies, if liked. Bake in the preheated oven for 12–15 minutes until lightly browned around the edges. Remove from the oven, leave on the cookie sheet for 2 minutes, and then transfer to a cooling rack to cool completely.

Faces: Pipe 2 large dots of white icing onto each cookie for eyes and push a mini candy-coated chocolate into the center of each eye. Use red decorator frosting to pipe eyebrows, noses, and mouths.

Hair: Beat yellow food coloring into the buttercream, adding a little at a time until the desired shade is reached. Put the buttercream in a paper pastry bag and snip off a thick tip so the buttercream flows out in a thick line. Use to pipe wavy hair around the sides of the cookies.

Ribbons: Pipe green decorator frosting over the buttercream on each cookie for ribbon and flower shapes, then pipe dots of white decorator frosting into the center of each flower.

Try me too! page 98

Crazy curls hair

Chocolate eyes

Big happy smile

Curled Flamingo

Ingredients

- 1 quantity chocolate cookie dough (see page 7)
- Flour, for dusting
- 1³/₄ oz (50 g) milk chocolate, melted (see page 16)
- 6 chocolate marshmallow cookies
- 13 oz (375 g) deep pink rolled fondant
- Confectioners' sugar, for dusting
- Yellow, orange, and black food coloring
- 1³/₄ oz (50 g) white rolled fondant

Equipment

- Large cookie sheet
- Rolling pin
- 3¹/₂-inch (8.5-cm) round cookie cutter
- Narrow-handled teaspoon
- Small sharp knife
- Fine paintbrush

Baking: Heat the oven to 375°F (190°C, Gas 6) and grease a large cookie sheet. Roll out the dough on a lightly floured surface until about ¹/₄ inch (5 mm) thick and cut out 6 cookies using a 3¹/₂-inch (8.5-cm) round cookie cutter. Place the dough rounds on the cookie sheet, spacing them well apart. Gather up the trimmings and reroll to make extra cookies, if liked. Bake in the preheated oven for 12–15 minutes until appear baked but are still slightly soft. Remove from the oven, leave on the cookie sheet for 2 minutes, and then transfer to a cooling rack to cool completely.

Bodies: Spread a little melted chocolate over the bases of the chocolate marshmallow cookies and position them on the cookies slightly off center. Working on a surface dusted with confectioners' sugar, knead a little yellow food coloring into the pink rolled fondant. (This isn't essential but gives the fondant a more realistic flamingo-like color). For each body, take a ³/₄ oz (20 g) piece of the fondant and flatten it into a round about 3¹/₄ inches (3 cm) in diameter. Mold the fondant over the cookie. Using the end of a narrow-handled teaspoon and the tip of a knife, press into the fondant to make indent markings.

Necks and heads: Roll a 1¹/₂ oz (40 g) piece of pink fondant under your fingers into a long sausage shape that is thick at one end, thinner through the middle section for the neck, and then thick again for the head. Cut a deep "v" shape out of the head end for the beak. Spoon a little more melted chocolate on the cookie beside the flamingo's body and position the neck and head. Curl it round so the head rests on the base of the neck, as in the picture. Repeat for the remaining cookies.

Beaks: For each flamingo, take a grape-sized ball of white fondant and mold it into a beak shape that will slot into the cut out "v" shape on the head. Push into position, securing with a dampened paintbrush. Dilute a little orange food colour with water and paint the central area of the beaks, as in the picture. Use black food coloring to paint the end of the beaks and eyes.

Finishing touches: Use the diluted orange food coloring to add highlights of color to the bodies. Thinly roll out the remaining white fondant and cut out tiny diamond shapes. Secure on the bodies with a dampened paintbrush for feathers.

Long curly neck

Beware the beak!

Fabulous feathers

Peacock

Ingredients

- 1 quantity ginger cookie dough (see page 7)
- Flour, for dusting
- 2$^1/_2$ oz (75 g) white chocolate, melted (see page 16)
- 7 oz (200 g) turquoise rolled fondant
- Confectioners' sugar, for dusting
- 3$^1/_2$ oz (100 g) blue rolled fondant
- 1$^3/_4$ oz (50 g) purple rolled fondant
- $^1/_2$ oz (15 g) white rolled fondant
- Black food coloring
- $^1/_2$ oz (15 g) orange rolled fondant

Equipment

- Large cookie sheet
- Parchment paper, for tracing
- Pencil
- Scissors
- Rolling pin
- Small sharp knife
- Paper pastry bag (see page 17)
- Small spatula
- Fine paintbrush

Baking: Heat the oven to 375°F (190°C, Gas 6). Grease a large cookie sheet and trace and cut out the peacock template on page 126. Roll out the dough on a lightly floured surface until about $^1/_4$ inch (5 mm) thick, then cut around the template to shape 6 cookies. Place the dough shapes on the cookie sheet, spacing them well apart. Gather up the trimmings and reroll to make extra cookies, if liked. Bake in the preheated oven for 12–15 minutes until lightly browned around the edges. Remove from the oven, leave on the cookie sheet for 2 minutes, and then transfer to a cooling rack to cool completely.

Bases: Put a few teaspoons of the melted chocolate in a paper piping, snip off the merest tip, and set aside. Using a small spatula, spread the remaining chocolate in a thin layer over the cookies. Roll out the turquoise rolled fondant on a surface dusted with confectioners' sugar until about $^1/_{16}$ inch (2 mm) thick, and cut around the peacock template. Repeat to give 6 bases. Place on the cookies, pressing down gently.

Bodies: Take large grape-sized pieces of blue fondant and mold into a pear shapes. Flatten slightly and position on the center of the bases, securing in place with a dampened paintbrush. Thinly roll out the purple fondant, then roll a toothpick along on edge so that it starts to frill (see page 14). Cut into tiny pieces and secure to the tops of the heads, as in the picture.

Feathers: Roll 54 tiny balls of blue fondant between your finger and thumb and flatten into an oval shape. Press gently onto the cookies to secure. Pipe blobs of white chocolate from the pastry bag onto the blue ovals. Shape smaller pieces of the remaining purple fondant and press gently into the chocolate.

Finishing touches: Use the white fondant to shape tiny eyes and secure in place. Use black food coloring and a fine paintbrush to paint the centers of the eyes. Use orange fondant to shape diamond shapes for beaks, as small as you can make them, and triangles for feet. Secure in place.

Fondant feathers

Perfect peacock paunch

Westie Dog

Ingredients

- 1 quantity chocolate cookie dough (see page 7)
- Flour, for dusting
- 3$\frac{1}{2}$ oz (100 g) white chocolate, melted (see page 16)
- 6 small round yellow candies
- 2$\frac{1}{2}$ oz (75 g) blue rolled fondant
- 2$\frac{1}{2}$ oz (75 g) green rolled fondant
- Confectioners' sugar, for dusting
- Small piece each of black and white rolled fondant
- Blue and red food coloring
- 6 small ribbon bows, ideally in green or blue check

Equipment

- Large cookie sheet
- Rolling pin
- 3-inch (7.5-cm) round cookie cutter
- 2 paper pastry bags (see page 17)
- Scissors
- Parchment paper
- Toothpick
- Small spatula
- Small sharp knife
- Fine paintbrush

Baking: Heat the oven to 375°F (190°C, Gas 6) and grease a large cookie sheet. Roll out the dough on a lightly floured surface until about $\frac{1}{4}$ inch (5 mm) thick and cut out 6 cookies using a 3-inch (7.5-cm) round cookie cutter. Place the dough rounds on the cookie sheet, spacing them well apart. Gather up the trimmings and reroll to make extra cookies, if liked. Bake in the preheated oven for 12–15 minutes until appear baked but are still slightly soft. Remove from the oven, leave on the cookie sheet for 2 minutes, and then transfer to a cooling rack to cool completely.

Balls: Put half the melted chocolate in a paper pastry bag and snip off the merest tip. Pipe a curved line on the yellow sweets to resemble tennis balls.

Dogs: Trace the dog template (see opposite) onto parchment paper. Repeat to give 8 Westie dogs (including a couple extra in case of breakages). Lay a second sheet of parchment paper over the traced outlines, then use the melted chocolate in the pastry bag to pipe the outlines of the Scottie dogs. Snip off more of the pastry bag tip and fill in the outlines, spreading the chocolate into the corners with a toothpick. Leave to set for several hours or overnight.

Grass and sky: Using a small spatula, spread the remaining melted chocolate in a thin layer over the cookies. Roll out the blue and green rolled fondants on a surface dusted with confectioners' sugar until about $\frac{1}{16}$ inch (2 mm) thick. Cut out 3 rounds from each color using a 3-inch (7.5-cm) round cookie cutter. Cut each round in half and use a semicircle of each color to cover the cookies.

Faces: Roll 6 tiny balls of black fondant between your finger and thumb into oval shapes and gently press onto the chocolate dogs for noses, securing with a dampened paintbrush if necessary. Roll 12 tiny balls of white fondant for eyes. Paint the centers of the eyes using a paintbrush and blue food coloring, and paint on a small mouth using red food coloring.

Assembling: Carefully peel the paper away from the dogs. Secure the dogs and balls to the cookies, using the melted chocolate in the pastry bag. (If the chocolate has set in the bag, soften it briefly in the microwave, see page 16). Secure the ribbon bows in place with dots of chocolate.

Cute bow

Let's play ball!

Festival Elephant

Ingredients

- 1 quantity vanilla cookie dough (see page 6)
- Flour, for dusting
- Blue food coloring
- 1 quantity vanilla buttercream (see page 10)
- $3^1/2$ oz (100 g) purple rolled fondant
- Confectioners' sugar, for dusting
- Gold dragées
- $1^3/4$ oz (50 g) red rolled fondant
- $1/2$ oz (15 g) blue rolled fondant

Equipment

- Large cookie sheet
- Parchment paper, for tracing
- Pencil
- Scissors
- Rolling pin
- Small sharp knife
- Paper pastry bag (see page 17)
- Fine round decorating tip
- Small spatula
- $1/2$-inch (1-cm) flower plunger or cookie cutter

Baking: Heat the oven to 375°F (190°C, Gas 6). Grease a large cookie sheet, and trace and cut out the elephant template on page 122. Roll out the dough on a lightly floured surface until about $1/4$ inch (5 mm) thick, then cut around the template to shape 6 cookies. Place the dough shapes on the cookie sheet, spacing them well apart. Gather up the trimmings and reroll to make extra cookies, if liked. Bake in the preheated oven for 12–15 minutes until lightly browned around the edges. Remove from the oven, leave on the cookie sheet for 2 minutes, and then transfer to a cooling rack to cool completely.

Costumes: Beat blue food coloring into the buttercream, adding a little at a time until the desired shade is reached. Put all but 1 tablespoon in a paper pastry bag fitted with a fine plain decorator tip. Spread the remaining buttercream over the elephant backs (where the blankets will be positioned), using a small spatula.

Trace and cut out the elephant's blanket and headpiece templates (see opposite). Roll out the purple fondant on a surface dusted with confectioners' sugar until about $1/16$ inch (2 mm) thick, and cut around the template. Repeat to give 6 blankets and headpieces. Secure the blankets in place, then dot a little buttercream from the pastry bag onto the tops of the heads and gently press the headpieces in place. Make diamond-shaped markings $1/2$ inch (1 cm) apart over the blankets with the back of a knife. Gently press gold dragées into the fondant while it is still soft.

Thinly roll out the red fondant and cut out eighteen $1/2$-inch (1-cm) wide strips. Secure around the blanket straight edges with buttercream from the pastry bag, trimming to fit at the corners. Secure thin bands of red fondant around the ankles.

Thinly roll out the blue fondant and cut out $^1/_2$-inch (1-cm) flower shapes using a plunger or cookie cutter. Secure onto the headpieces with a dampened paintbrush, trimming off the excess.

Finishing touches: Use the buttercream in the pastry bag to pipe lines of beading on the bodies, trunk, and around the legs (see page 19). Secure more gold dragées over the legs and onto the headpieces.

Beautiful blanket

Bling, bling

Fish

Ingredients

- 1 quantity ginger cookie dough (see page 7)
- Flour, for dusting
- 4$\frac{1}{2}$ oz (125 g) blue rolled fondant
- Confectioners' sugar, for dusting
- 1 quantity vanilla buttercream (see page 10)
- 3$\frac{1}{2}$ oz (100 g) white rolled fondant
- Orange, black, and blue food coloring

Equipment

- Large cookie sheet
- Rolling pin
- 3-inch (7.5-cm) round cookie cutter
- Parchment paper, for tracing
- Pencil
- Scissors
- Craft knife
- Fine paintbrush

Baking: Heat the oven to 375°F (190°C, Gas 6) and grease a large cookie sheet. Roll out the dough on a lightly floured surface until about $\frac{1}{4}$ inch (5 mm) thick and cut out 6 cookies using a 3-inch (7.5-cm) round cookie cutter. Place the dough rounds on the cookie sheet, spacing them well apart. Gather up the trimmings and reroll to make extra cookies, if liked. Bake in the preheated oven for 12–15 minutes until lightly browned around the edges. Remove from the oven, leave on the cookie sheet for 2 minutes, and then transfer to a cooling rack to cool completely.

Sea: Roll out the blue rolled fondant on a surface dusted with confectioners' sugar and cut out six 3-inch (7.5-cm) rounds using the cookie cutter. Using a small spatula, spread the cookies with the buttercream, leaving an $\frac{1}{2}$-inch (1-cm) edge. Position the blue fondant rounds on top, pressing the edges down gently.

Fish: Trace and cut out the fish template (see opposite). Roll out the white until about $\frac{1}{16}$ inch (2 mm) thick, and cut around the template. Repeat to give 6 fish. Secure the templates in place with a dampened paintbrush. Dilute a little orange and black food coloring with water and use to paint the fish markings and face, as in the picture.

Bubbles: Roll 24 balls of white fondant between your finger and thumb and secure in place. Dilute the blue food colouring with water and paint little blue lines onto the bubbles.

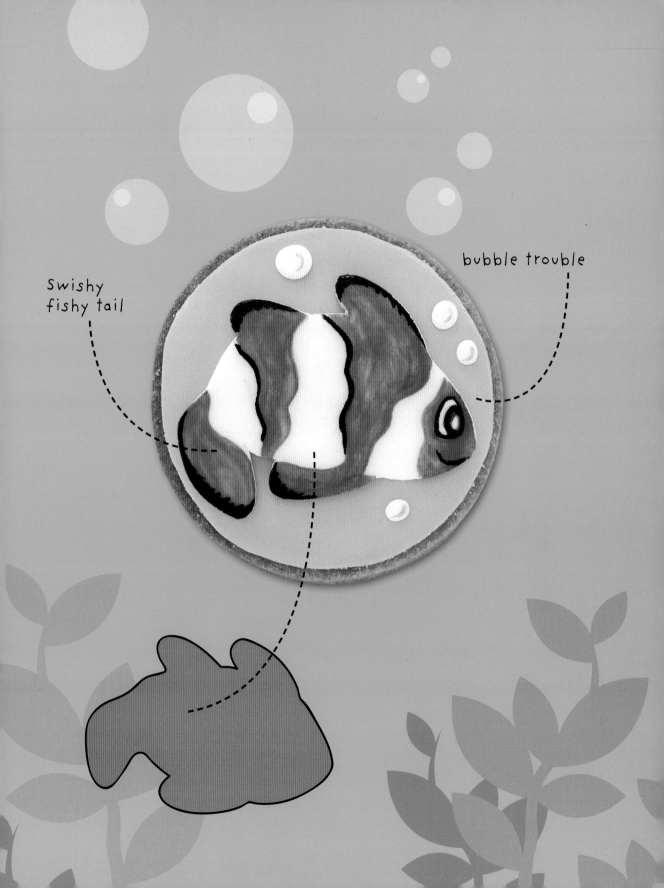

Swishy
fishy tail

bubble trouble

Chubby Owl

Ingredients

- 1 quantity chocolate cookie dough (see page 7)
- Flour, for dusting
- 2 quantities chocolate buttercream (see page 10)
- $3^{1}/_{2}$ oz (100 g) semisweet chocolate, melted (see page 16)
- 12 flat white candies
- 12 purple mini round candies
- 2 orange fruit chews
- 4 pink square fruit chews

Equipment

- Large cookie sheet
- Rolling pin
- $3^{1}/_{2}$-inch (8.5-cm) round cookie cutter
- Small spatula
- Small decorating tip
- Paper pastry bag (see page 17)
- Scissors

Baking: Heat the oven to 375°F (190°C, Gas 6) and grease a large cookie sheet. Roll out the dough on a lightly floured surface until about $^{1}/_{4}$ inch (5 mm) thick and cut out 6 cookies using a $3^{1}/_{2}$-inch (8.5-cm) round cookie cutter. Place the dough rounds on the cookie sheet, spacing them well apart. Gather up the trimmings and reroll to make extra cookies, if liked. Bake in the preheated oven for 12–15 minutes until appear baked but are still slightly soft. Remove from the oven, leave on the cookie sheet for 2 minutes, and then transfer to a cooling rack to cool completely.

Plumages: Spread a little buttercream over the cookies using a small spatula, doming it up slightly in the center. Use the wide end of a decorating tip to impress semicircular shapes down the center of the buttercream.

Eyes: Put the melted chocolate in a paper pastry bag and snip off the merest tip. Push 2 flat white candies into each cookie, then secure the purple mini round candies in the centers with dots of melted chocolate. Squeeze further dots of chocolate onto the sweets as pupils.

Wings and heads: Pipe wing outlines and the tops of the heads with the melted chocolate, as in the photograph. Fill in the outlines with more chocolate.

Beaks and feet: Soften the orange fruit chews in the microwave for a few seconds (see page 20). Break off pea-sized pieces and shape beaks. Press into the buttercream. For the feet, soften the pink chews and break into small pieces. Flatten the pieces and cut 3 notches into each with scissors. Press onto the buttercream and pipe on claws with more chocolate.

twitttttwwwooooooooo

Smells scrummy

Naughty night-time snack!

See who else can fly...

Dragonfly

Ingredients

- 1 quantity vanilla cookie dough (see page 6)
- Flour, for dusting
- 1 quantity royal icing (see page 11)
- Lilac and blue food coloring
- 1 quantity vanilla buttercream (see page 10)
- $4^1/_2$ oz (125 g) green rolled fondant
- Confectioners' sugar, for dusting
- $1^3/_4$ oz (50 g) purple rolled fondant
- $1^3/_4$ oz (50 g) lilac rolled fondant
- 6 blue small jelly beans

Equipment

- Large cookie sheet
- Rolling pin
- 3-inch (7.5 cm) round cookie cutter
- Parchment paper, for tracing
- Pencil
- 4 paper pastry bags (see page 17)
- Fine round decorating tip
- Scissors
- Toothpick
- Small spatula

Baking: Heat the oven to 375°F (190°C, Gas 6) and grease a large cookie sheet. Roll out the dough on a lightly floured surface until about $^1/_4$ inch (5 mm) thick and cut out 6 cookies using a 3-inch (7.5-cm) round cookie cutter. Place the dough rounds on the cookie sheet, spacing them well apart. Gather up the trimmings and reroll to make extra cookies, if liked. Bake in the preheated oven for 12–15 minutes until lightly browned around the edges. Remove from the oven, leave on the cookie sheet for 2 minutes, and then transfer to a cooling rack to cool completely.

Wings: Trace the wings template (see opposite) onto parchment paper. Repeat to give 8 set of wings (including a couple extra in case of breakages). Lay a second sheet of parchment paper over the traced outlines. Beat lilac food coloring into one-third of the royal icing, adding a little at a time until the desired shade is reached. Put in a paper pastry bag fitted with a fine round decorating tip, then pipe the outlines of the wing.

Put 2 tablespoons of the royal icing in a separate paper pastry bag and set aside. Add a little blue food coloring and a dash of water to the remaining royal icing to give a thinner consistency (see page 19). Put the icing in another paper pastry bag and snip about $^1/_4$ inch (5 mm) off the tip. Thin the lilac royal icing used for piping the wing outlines with water to the same consistency as the blue royal icing. Put in a new pastry bag and snip off the merest tip. Fill in the outlined areas of the wings with blue royal icing, spreading it into the corners with a toothpick, then pipe on dots and splashes with the thinned lilac royal. Leave to set for several hours or overnight.

Grass: Spread a little buttercream over each cookie using a small spatula. Roll out the green fondant on a surface dusted with confectioners' sugar until about $1/16$ inch (2 mm) thick, and cut out 6 rounds with the 3-inch (7.5cm) cookie cutter. Position a round on each cookie.

Bodies: Once the wings have set, use the purple and lilac fondants to shape dragonfly bodies. Start by molding grape-sized pieces of black fondant into oval shapes. Press them onto the green fondant. Add small pieces of fondant in alternating colors to shape the bodies, finishing with pointed tails shaped from black fondant. Cut off the tips of the jelly beans and press them into the heads for eyes.

Assembling: Cut the merest tip off the pastry bag of uncolored royal icing. Push small holes into the heads on either side and pipe a little royal icing into each. Carefully peel the paper away from the wings and gently push the winds into position. (If necessary support the wings with small balls of paper towel until the royal icing sets.)

Fluttering floating fondant

Trophy

Ingredients

- 1 quantity lemon cookie dough (see page 7)
- Flour, for dusting
- 1 egg white, beaten
- 1 quantity royal icing (see page 11)
- Yellow food coloring
- Lemon juice, for thinning
- 1 quantity chocolate buttercream (see page 10)
- $1^3/_4$ oz (50 g) red rolled fondant
- Confectioners' sugar, for dusting
- $^1/_2$ oz (15 g) white rolled fondant
- Black food coloring

Equipment

- 2 large cookie sheets
- Rolling pin
- 3-inch and $^3/_4$-inch (7.5-cm and 2-cm) round cookie cutters
- Small sharp knife
- Fine paintbrush
- 3 paper pastry bags (see page 17)
- Fine round decorating tip
- Toothpick

Baking: Heat the oven to 375°F (190°C, Gas 6) and grease 2 large cookie sheets. Roll out the dough on a lightly floured surface until about $^1/_4$ inch (5 mm) thick. Cut out 3 rounds using a 3-inch (7.5-cm) cookie cutter and six 2 x $1^1/_2$-inches (5 x 3.5-cm) rectangles from the dough. Cut the rounds in half and then lightly roll each semicircle to lengthen it slightly into a cup shape. Reroll the trimmings and cut out six $^3/_4$-inch (2-cm) rounds, and lightly roll each of these to shape into ovals for the trophy stems. Cut out twelve 2 x $^1/_2$-inches (5 x 1-cm) strips from the remaining dough for the handles. Assemble all these shapes into "trophies" on the cookie sheets, bending the long strips into curves for handles. Brush a little egg white over the edges of dough that are to be connected, using a fine paintbrush, then firmly push the pieces together at the join. Bake in the preheated oven for 12–15 minutes until lightly browned around the edges. Remove from the oven, leave on the cookie sheet for 5 minutes, and then transfer to a cooling rack to cool completely.

Trophies: Put 1–2 tablespoons of the royal icing in a paper pastry bag fitted with a fine round decorating tip. Use to pipe outlines around the edges of the trophy cup shapes and then around the trophy bases. Add a little yellow food coloring and a few drops of lemon juice to the remaining royal icing to give a thinner consistency (see page 19). Put the icing in a second paper pastry bag and snip $^1/_4$ inch (5 mm) off the tip. Pipe the icing inside the outlined areas of the trophies, spreading it into the corners with a toothpick.

Bases: Put the chocolate buttercream into another pastry bag and snip off the tip. Use to pipe thick lines, back and forth, over the bases. Leave to set for several hours or overnight.

HURRAH! BRAVO!

Rosettes: Roll out the red rolled fondant on a surface dusted with confectioners' sugar until about $1/16$ inch (2 mm) thick. Cut out $5/8$-inch (1.5-cm) wide strips, each about 4 inches (10 cm) long. Starting at one end of a fondant strip, fold along one long edge so it starts to curl round into a rosette shape. Pinch the ends together. Repeat to give 6 rosettes. Cut 12 ribbon ends from the trimmings and secure in place on the cookies with a dampened paintbrush. Press the rosettes gently on top. For the rosette centers, roll 6 pea-sized pieces of white fondant between your finger and thumb, then flatten until about $1/2$ inch (1 cm) in diameter. Secure in place with a dampened paintbrush. Use a fine paintbrush and black food coloring to paint a number "1" onto the white fondant.

Paint Palette

Ingredients

- 1 quantity ginger cookie dough (see page 7)
- Flour, for dusting
- 12–15 hard fruit candies
- 6 red licorice sticks, ideally smooth edged
- Tube of white and red decorator frosting

Equipment

- Large cookie sheet
- Baking parchment
- Pencil
- Scissors
- Rolling pin
- $3/4$-inch (2-cm) round cookie cutter
- Small tray
- Craft knife

Baking: Heat the oven to 375°F (190°C, Gas 6). Grease a large cookie sheet, and trace and cut out the paint palette template on page 124. Roll out the dough on a lightly floured surface until about $1/4$ inch (5 mm) thick, then cut around the template to shape 6 cookies. Place the dough shapes on the cookie sheet, spacing them slightly apart. Gather up the trimmings and reroll to make extra cookies, if liked. Using a $3/4$-inch (2-cm) round cookie cutter, cut 6–7 holes in the cookies. Using you finger, slightly elongate the middle hole on each cookie. Bake in the preheated oven for 5 minutes.

Paint: While the cookies are baking, lightly crush the hard fruit candy, while they are still in their wrappers, using a rolling pin. Remove the cookies from the oven and position a few pieces of crushed candy in each of the paint holes. Return to the oven for a further 7–10 minutes until lightly browned around the edges and the candies have melted. Leave the cookies on the cookie sheet for 5-6 minutes until the sweets are brittle, then transfer to a cooling rack to cool completely.

Paintbrushes: Cut the licorice sticks into $4^1/4$-inch (11-cm) lengths, and place on a small, parchment-lined tray. Use white decorator frosting to pipe on the paintbrush tips. This is easiest done by building up the tip area with squiggly piping and then piping horizontal lines over the top starting at the base of the "brush" and trailing off at the tip. Leave to set for several hours or overnight. (As a shortcut, secure the licorice directly on the paint palette with a few small dots of white or red decorator frosting and pipe on the brush head. This way you won't have to wait for the brush heads to harden).

Try me too! page 96

Lovely licorice paintbrush

Finishing touches: Use the white decorator frosting to pipe a line around the edges of the cookies and around the central hole. Carefully rest the paintbrushes on top, securing with a few dots of decorator frosting.

Candy paint

Artfully created

Topiary Tree

Ingredients

- 1 quantity vanilla cookie dough (see page 6)
- Flour, for dusting
- Blue and green food colorings
- 2 quantities vanilla buttercream (see page 10)
- 1 oz (25 g) plain chocolate, melted (see page 16)
- 6 orange square fruit chews
- 1–2 red licorice laces

Equipment

- Large cookie sheet
- Rolling pin
- $3^1/2$-inch (8.5-cm) round cookie cutter
- Small spatula
- 2 paper pastry bags (see page 17)
- Leaf decorating tip
- Parchment paper, for tracing
- Pencil
- Scissors
- Craft knife

Baking: Heat the oven to 375°F (190°C, Gas 6) and grease a large cookie sheet. Roll out the dough on a lightly floured surface until about $1/4$ inch (5 mm) thick and cut out 6 cookies using a $3^1/2$-inch (8.5-cm) round cookie cutter. Place the dough rounds on the cookie sheet, spacing them slightly apart. Gather up the trimmings and reroll to make extra cookies, if liked. Bake in the preheated oven for 12–15 minutes until lightly browned around the edges. Remove from the oven, leave on the cookie sheet for 2 minutes, and then transfer to a cooling rack to cool completely.

Bases: Beat blue food coloring into the one-third of the buttercream, adding a little at a time until the desired shade is reached. Using a small spatula, spread the buttercream over the cookies in a thin layer. Scrape off any buttercream that extends over the edges.

Tree trunks: Put the melted chocolate in a paper pastry bag and snip off the merest tip. Use to pipe several lines down the center of the cookies to shape trunks that are about $1/2$ inch (1 cm) wide and $1^1/4$ inches (3 cm) long.

Foliage: Beat green food coloring into the remaining buttercream, adding a little at a time until the desired shade is reached. Put in a paper pastry bag fitted with a leaf decorating tip (these should be about 2 inches (5 cm) in diameter). On each cookie, pipe a circle of leaves to shape the outer edges of the foliage by squeezing a little icing out of the bag and releasing the pressure as you pull the bag away. Continue to build up the centers of the trees by adding more circles of leaves until you reach the middle.

Pots: Trace and cut out the pot template (see above). Using a rolling pin, flatten the fruit chews until a similar size to the pot template. Lay the template over a chew and cut around with scissors. Impress a rim line near the top of the pot, using the back of a knife, then press into position. Repeat to give 6 pots. Cut short lengths of licorice lace and use to shape bows at the tops of the pots.

Chewy licorice bow

Ace of Hearts

Ingredients

- 1 quantity vanilla cookie dough (see page 6)
- Flour, for dusting
- 1 quantity vanilla buttercream (see page 10)
- $5^1/_2$ oz (150 g) white rolled fondant
- Confectioners' sugar, for dusting
- $1^3/_4$ oz (50 g) red rolled fondant
- Black and red food coloring

Equipment

- Large cookie sheet
- Rolling pin
- Small spatula
- Small sharp knife
- $1^1/_4$-inch and $^1/_2$-inch (3-cm and 1-cm) heart cookie cutters
- Fine paintbrush
- Paper pastry bag (see page 17)
- Fine round decorating tip

Baking: Heat the oven to 375°F (190°C, Gas 6) and grease a large cookie sheet. Roll out the dough on a lightly floured surface until about $^1/_4$ inch (5 mm) thick and cut out six $3^1/_2$ x $2^1/_2$-inch (9 x 6-cm) rectangles. Place the dough shapes on the cookie sheet, spacing them slightly apart. Gather up the trimmings and reroll to make extra cookies, if liked. Bake in the preheated oven for 12–15 minutes until lightly browned around the edges. Remove from the oven, leave on the cookie sheet for 2 minutes, and then transfer to a cooling rack to cool completely.

Bases: Using a small spatula, spread the cookies with a little buttercream, leaving a $^1/_2$-inch (1-cm) edge. Roll out the white rolled fondant on a surface dusted with confectioners' sugar until about $^1/_{16}$ inch (2 mm) thick and cut out rectangles that are slightly smaller than the dimensions of the cookies. Arrange in position, pressing down gently around the edges.

Hearts: Roll out the red rolled fondant until about $^1/_{16}$ inch (2 mm) thick. Cut out 6 heart shapes using an $1^1/_4$-inch (3-cm) heart cookie cutter and place on the cookies in the center, securing with a dampened paintbrush. Cut out 12 smaller hearts using a $^1/_2$-inch (1-cm) heart cookie cutter. Position one heart near each of the corners of the cookies, leaving enough space to add in the "A", as in the picture.

Finishing touches: Dilute a little black food coloring with water then, using a fine paintbrush, paint an "A" above each small heart. Beat red food coloring into the remaining buttercream, adding a little at a time until the desired shade is reached. Put in a paper pastry bag fitted with a fine round decorating tip, then pipe beading (see page 19) around the edges of the white fondant.

Snap! Snap! Snaaaaaap!

Ace of hearts

I love cookies

Fancy frosting

Trainers

Ingredients

- 1 quantity ginger cookie dough (see page 7)
- Flour, for dusting
- 1³/₄ oz (50 g) white rolled fondant
- Confectioners' sugar, for dusting
- Tube of black decorator frosting
- Length of red chewy fruit roll
- 6 red flat chewy candies, about 1¹/₄ inches (3 cm) in diameter, or gummy candy drops

Equipment

- Large cookie sheet
- Rolling pin
- Parchment, for tracing
- Pencil
- Scissors
- Small sharp knife
- 1¹/₄-inch (3-cm) star cookie cutter

Baking: Heat the oven to 375°F (190°C, Gas 6). Grease a large cookie sheet, and trace and cut out the trainer template on page 127. Roll out the dough on a lightly floured surface until about ¹/₄ inch (5 mm) thick. Cut around the template to shape 6 cookies. Place the dough shapes on the cookie sheet, spacing them slightly apart. Gather up the trimmings and reroll to make extra cookies, if liked. Bake in the preheated oven for 12–15 minutes until lightly browned around the edges. Remove from the oven, leave on the cookie sheet for 2 minutes, and then transfer to a cooling rack to cool completely.

Soles and toe caps: Roll out the white rolled fondant on a surface dusted with confectioners' sugar until about ¹/₁₆ inch (2 mm) thick. Cut out strips about 4 x ¹/₂ inches (10 x 1 cm) long. Pipe a line of black decorator frosting along the bases of the cookies and secure the fondant strips in place bending them slightly to fit. Cut out the dotted line area of the trainer template. Place on the white rolled fondant and cut out the template. Repeat to give 6 toe caps. Secure in place with the decorator frosting. Reserve the white fondant trimmings.

Piping: Use black decorator frosting to pipe outlines around the edges of the cookies and along the sole, as in the picture.

Laces: Roll 30 tiny balls of white fondant between your finger and thumb and flatten. Arrange 5 pieces down the front of each trainer, securing in place with a little decorator frosting. Cut thin strips of the red chewy fruit roll and position for laces, securing in place by pressing the ends into the white fondant.

Stars: Secure the flat red chews to the heels with decorator frosting. If using candy drops, soften very briefly in the microwave (see page 20) and flatten with a rolling pin until about $1^1/_4$ inches (3 cm) in diameter. Thinly roll out the white fondant trimmings and cut out 5 star shapes using an $1^1/_4$-inch (3 cm) star cookie cutter. Secure to the red sweets.

Luscious laces

Chewy star

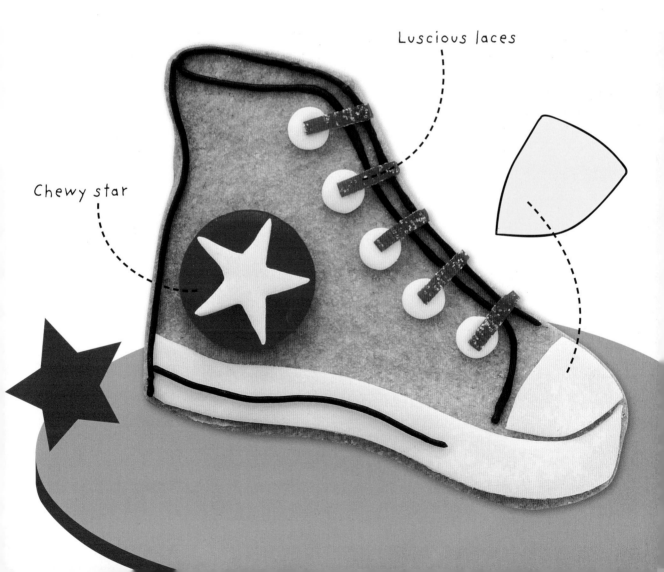

Pink Heart

Ingredients

- 1 quantity vanilla cookie dough (see page 6)
- Flour, for dusting
- 1 quantity vanilla buttercream (see page 10)
- 7 oz (200 g) deep pink rolled fondant
- $1^3/_4$ oz (50 g) pale pink rolled fondant
- Confectioners' sugar, for dusting
- Pink food coloring

Equipment

- Large cookie sheet
- Rolling pin
- $3^1/_4$-inch, $5/_8$-inch, and $1/_2$-inch (8-cm, 1.5-cm, and 1-cm) heart cookie cutters
- Small spatula
- Paper pastry bag (see page 17)
- Fine round decorating tip

Baking: Heat the oven to 375°F (190°C, Gas 6) and grease a large cookie sheet. Roll out the dough on a lightly floured surface until about $1/_4$ inch (5 mm) thick and cut out 6 cookies using a $3^1/_4$-inch (8-cm) heart cookie cutter. Place the dough rounds on the cookie sheet, spacing them slightly apart. Gather up the trimmings and reroll to make extra cookies, if liked. Bake in the preheated oven for 12–15 minutes until lightly browned around the edges. Remove from the oven, leave on the cookie sheet for 2 minutes, and then transfer to a cooling rack to cool completely.

Hearts: Using a small spatula, spread the cookies with the buttercream, leaving a $1/_2$-inch (1-cm) edge. Roll out the deep pink rolled fondant on a surface dusted with confectioners' sugar until about $1/_{16}$ inch (2 mm) thick. Roll out the pale pink fondant to the same thickness, and cut out heart shapes using $5/_8$-inch (1.5-cm) and $1/_2$-inch (1-cm) heart cookie cutters. Arrange the hearts over the deep pink fondant, leaving a $1/_2$-inch (1-cm) space between each. Gently roll a rolling pin over the fondant until the heart shapes are pressed into the deep pink fondant but still retain their shape. Using the $3^1/_4$-inch (8-cm) heart cookie cutter, cut out 6 hearts and lay them over the cookies, pressing the fondant down gently around the edges.

Beading: Beat pink food coloring into the remaining buttercream, adding a little at a time until the desired shade is reached. Put in a paper pastry bag fitted with a fine round decorator tip, then pipe beaded lines (see page 19) around the edges of the fondant.

Fabulous, fancy fondant

Yummy hearts

Spread the cookie **love!**

It was love at first sight

See what the Easter bunny brought... ☞

Easter Basket

Ingredients

- 1 quantity chocolate cookie dough (see page 7)
- Flour, for dusting
- 2$\frac{1}{2}$ oz (75 g) white chocolate, melted (see page 16)
- A handful of small pastel-colored jelly beans

Equipment

- Large cookie sheet
- Rolling pin
- Paper pastry bag (see page 17)
- Scissors

Baking: Heat the oven to 375°F (190°C, Gas 6) and grease a large cookie sheet. Roll out the dough on a lightly floured surface until about $\frac{1}{4}$ inch (5 mm) thick and cut out six 3$\frac{1}{2}$ x 2$\frac{1}{2}$-inch (8 x 6-cm) rectangles. Place the dough shapes on the cookie sheet, spacing them slightly apart. Gather up the trimmings and reroll to make extra cookies, if liked. Bake in the preheated oven for 12–15 minutes until the cookies appear baked but are still slightly soft. Remove from the oven, leave on the cookie sheet for 2 minutes, and then transfer to a cooling rack to cool completely.

Baskets: Put the melted chocolate in a paper pastry bag and snip off the merest tip. Use to pipe a simple basket outline onto the lower half of the cookies. To fill in the centers, scribble first vertical lines and then diagonal lines inside the basket area. (Be careful not to pipe so much chocolate that the cookie doesn't show through.) Pipe a semicircle of chocolate onto the cookies for the handles.

Eggs: Half fill the area above the basket and below the handle on each cookie with piped chocolate, then arrange the jelly beans on top. Use additional chocolate to secure any jelly beans that you position over the first layer of jelly beans. Leave to set for several hours or overnight.

Try me too! page 106

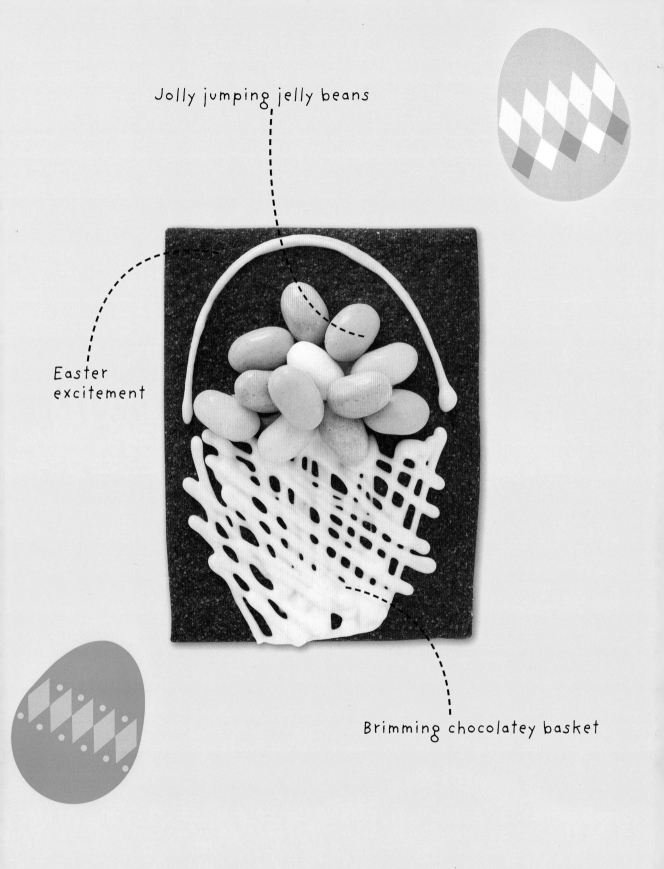

Jolly jumping jelly beans

Easter excitement

Brimming chocolatey basket

Birthday Cake

Ingredients

- 1 quantity vanilla cookie dough (see page 6)
- Flour, for dusting
- 1 egg white, beaten
- Pink food coloring
- 2 quantities vanilla buttercream (see page 10)
- Pink pearlescent dragées
- 6 pink square fruit chews
- 2 orange square fruit chews
- Plenty of mini lilac candy-coated chocolates

Equipment

- 2 large cookie sheets
- Rolling pin
- Small sharp knife
- Fine paintbrush
- Large pastry bag
- Star decorating tip
- Small spatula

Baking: Heat the oven to 375°F (190°C, Gas 6) and grease 2 large cookie sheets. Roll out the dough on a lightly floured surface until about $^1/_4$ inch (5 mm) thick and cut out six $3^1/_2$ x $2^1/_2$-inch (9 x 6-cm) rectangles. Place 3 dough shapes on each cookie sheet, spacing them well apart. Gather up the trimmings and reroll. Cut out 18 small rectangles, each measuring $1^1/_4$ x $^1/_4$ inches (30 x 5 mm). Brush a little egg white along one end of each of the smaller rectangles, using a fine paint brush, then firmly push them against a longer side of the larger rectangles to form candles. You want 3 candles per cake. Bake in the preheated oven for 12–15 minutes until lightly browned around the edges. Remove from the oven, leave on the cookie sheet for 5 minutes, and then transfer to a cooling rack to cool completely.

Icing the cakes: Beat pink food coloring into half of the buttercream, adding a little at a time until the desired shade is reached. Put in a large pastry bag fitted with a star decorating tip and set aside. Use a small spatula to spread a thin layer of the uncolored buttercream over the cakes. Arrange scallops of pink pearlescent dragées over the buttercream, as in the picture.

Candles: Dot a little buttercream along the candles to keep the decorations in place. Soften the pink fruit chews in the microwave for a few seconds if too firm to mold (see page 20). Flatten the chews with a rolling pin, then cut into 18 thin strips and press into position for candles. Soften the orange fruit chews in the same way, then break off small pieces and mold into flame shapes. Position the flames at the tops of the candles.

Hip hip hooray!

Finishing touches: Using the pink buttercream in the pastry bag, pipe along the base and tops of the cakes. Push small candy-coated chocolates into the buttercream along the tops of the cakes.

Beautiful birthday beads

Perfect piping

Baby Booties

Ingredients

- 1 quantity vanilla cookie dough (see page 6)
- Flour, for dusting
- 1 quantity royal icing (see page 11)
- Lemon juice, for thinning
- Large pink candy sprinkles
- 1 oz (25 g) pale pink rolled fondant
- Confectioners' sugar, for dusting

Equipment

- Large cookie sheet
- Parchment paper
- Pencil
- Scissors
- Rolling pin
- Fine paintbrush
- 2 paper pastry bags (see page 17)
- Fine round decorating tip
- Toothpick
- $^3/_8$-inch (8-mm) and $^1/_2$-inch (1-cm) flower plunger or cookie cutters

Baking: Grease a large cookie sheet. Trace and cut out the baby bootie template (see page 127) and the bootie center template (see opposite). Roll out the dough on a lightly floured surface until about $^1/_4$ inch (5 mm) thick, then cut around the bootie templates to shape 6 cookies. Place the dough shapes on the cookie sheet, spacing them slightly apart. Gather up the trimmings, reroll, and cut out the bootie center template to shape 12 cookies. Place 2 centers on each shoe, as in the iced areas in the picture.

Straps: Roll out any remaining trimmings and cut out $^1/_2$-inch (1-cm) strips. Cut the strips into 12 smaller $1^3/_4$-inch (4.5-cm) lengths and gently press 2 straps onto each cookie, as in the picture. Press the end of a paintbrush handled into the straps to make 4 holes along each. Bake in the preheated oven for 12–15 minutes until lightly browned around the edges. Remove from the oven, leave on the cookie sheet for 5 minutes, then transfer to a cooling rack to cool completely.

Booties: Put 3–4 tablespoons of the royal icing in a paper pastry bag fitted with a fine round decorating tip. Use to pipe outlines over the inner-shoe shapes and around the straps. Add a few drops of lemon juice to the remaining icing to give a thinner consistency (see page 19), then put the icing in a separate paper pastry bag and snip $^1/_4$ inch (5 mm) off the tip. Pipe the icing inside the outlined inner-sole areas, spreading it out with a toothpick. Pipe further lines around the edges of the cookies. Pipe a large dot of icing at the outside end of each strap and secure pink candy sprinkles to make fasteners.

Flowers: Roll out the pale pink rolled fondant on a surface dusted with confectioners' sugar until about $^1/_{16}$ inch (2 mm) thick. Cutting out 1 flower at a time and securing in place with dots of royal icing from the pastry bag, cut out 4 tiny flower shapes per cookie using a $^3/_8$-inch (8-mm) flower plunger or cookie cutter. Using a larger $^1/_2$-inch (1-cm) flower cutter, cut out and position 2 bigger flowers per cookie. Pipe dots of icing into the flower centers and around the flowers. Leave the cookies to set for several hours or overnight.

These booties are made for eating!

Fabulous flowers

Mortarboard

Ingredients

- 1 quantity ginger cookie dough (see page 7)
- Flour, for dusting
- 7 oz (200 g) red rolled fondant
- Confectioners' sugar, for dusting
- Tube of black decorator frosting
- Green sugar sprinkles (see page 21)
- 1 quantity vanilla buttercream (see page 10)
- 3^1/$_2$ oz (100 g) white rolled fondant
- Small piece black rolled fondant

Equipment

- Large cookie sheet
- Rolling pin
- 3-inch (7.5-cm) round cookie cutter
- Small tray
- Parchment paper
- Small spatula
- Craft knife

Baking: Heat the oven to 375°F (190°C, Gas 6) and grease a large cookie sheet. Roll out the dough on a lightly floured surface until about ^{1}/$_4$ inch (5 mm) thick and cut out 6 cookies using a 3-inch (7.5-cm) round cookie cutter. Place the dough rounds on the cookie sheet, spacing them slightly apart. Gather up the trimmings and reroll to make extra cookies, if liked. Bake in the preheated oven for 12–15 minutes until lightly browned around the edges. Remove from the oven, leave on the cookie sheet for 2 minutes, and then transfer to a cooling rack to cool completely.

Mortarboards: Line a small tray with baking parchment. Roll out half the red rolled fondant on a surface dusted with confectioners' sugar until about ^{1}/$_{16}$ inch (2 mm) thick. Cut out 1^3/$_4$-inch (4.5-cm) squares and place on the paper. Leave to set for several hours or overnight. When the squares are set, take a further 1^1/$_2$ oz (40 g) of the red fondant and shape into 3 cylinder shapes, about 1^1/$_4$ inches (3 cm) in diameter. Slice diagonally in half to shape 2 mortarboard bases. Secure a flat square to a flat end of each base with a few dots of black decorator.

Grass: Put the sugar sprinkles on a plate. Using a small spatula, spread the cookies with a thin layer of buttercream. Invert the cookies onto the sugar and press down gently so the sugar sticks.

Certificates: Roll out the white rolled fondant until about ^{1}/$_{16}$ inch (2 mm) thick. Cut out six 2-inch (5 cm) squares and roll up. Roll small pieces of black and burgundy fondant under your fingers until about ^{1}/$_8$ inch (3 mm) thick. Twist together into 6 ropes and wrap loosely around the certificates.

Assembling: Place the mortarboards and certificates on the cookies, securing with a little black decorator frosting. Use black decorator frosting to pipe tassels from the centers of the mortarboards and down the sides.

Sparkly sugar grass

Graduation celebration

Yummy scrummy scroll

Bollywood

Ingredients

- 1 quantity vanilla cookie dough (see page 6)
- Flour, for dusting
- Red food coloring
- 1 quantity vanilla buttercream (see page 10)
- 4 oz (125 g) red rolled fondant
- Confectioners' sugar, for dusting
- $2^{1}/_{2}$ oz (75 g) orange rolled fondant
- Gold dragées

Equipment

- Large cookie sheet
- Rolling pin
- 3-inch (7.5-cm) round cookie cutter
- Small spatula
- Parchment paper, for tracing
- Pencil
- Scissors
- Craft knife
- Fine paintbrush
- Paper pastry bag (see page 17)
- Fine round decorating tip

Baking: Heat the oven to 375°F (190°C, Gas 6) and grease a large cookie sheet. Roll out the dough on a lightly floured surface until about $^{1}/_{4}$ inch (5 mm) thick and cut out 6 cookies using a $3^{1}/_{2}$-inch (8.5-cm) round cookie cutter. Place the dough rounds on the cookie sheet, spacing them slightly apart. Gather up the trimmings and reroll to make extra cookies, if liked. Bake in the preheated oven for 12–15 minutes until lightly browned around the edges. Remove from the oven, leave on the cookie sheet for 2 minutes, and then transfer to a cooling rack to cool completely.

Bases: Beat red food coloring into the buttercream, adding a little at a time until the desired shade is reached, then spread a thin layer over the cookies with a small spatula. Roll out the red rolled fondant on a surface dusted with confectioners' sugar until about $^{1}/_{16}$ inch (2 mm) thick and cut out 6 circles with the 3-inch (7.5-cm) round cookie cutter. Position the circles on the cookies, pressing down gently around the edges.

Motifs: Trace and cut out the teardrop motif template (see opposite). Roll out the orange rolled fondant until about $^{1}/_{16}$ inch (2 mm) thick, then cut around the template. Repeat to give 18 motifs. Position 3 shapes on each cookie, securing in place with a dampened paintbrush.

Finishing touches: Put the remaining buttercream in a paper pastry bag fitted with a fine round decorating tip. Pipe lines around the edges of the motifs and dots in and around the motifs. Secure gold dragées to some of the dots. Pipe beading (see page 19) around the edges of the cookies.

Beautiful beads

Crazy colors

Turn over for some festive fun...

Pumpkin Pie

Ingredients

- 1 quantity ginger cookie dough (see page 7)
- Flour, for dusting
- 1 egg white, beaten
- 5 1/2 oz (150 g) fondant confectioners' sugar
- 2 tablespoons orange juice
- Orange food coloring
- Unsweetened cocoa powder, for dusting

Equipment

- Large cookie sheet
- Rolling pin
- 3-inch (7.5-cm) round cookie cutter
- Small sharp knife
- Paintbrush
- Toothpick

Baking: Heat the oven to 375°F (190°C, Gas 6) and grease a large cookie sheet. Roll out the dough on a lightly floured surface until about 1/4 inch (5 mm) thick and cut out 6 cookies using a 3-inch (7.5-cm) round cookie cutter. Place the dough rounds on the cookie sheet, spacing them well apart. Gather up the trimmings and reroll. Cut the dough into 1/2-inch (1-cm) wide strips, then cut across the strips diagonally to make diamond shapes. Use the tip of a sharp knife to make indents along the center of each diamond. Brush the edges of the cookies with egg white, using a paintbrush, and arrange the shapes to resemble leaves, as in the picture. Bake in the preheated oven for 12–15 minutes until lightly browned around the edges. Remove from the oven, leave on the cookie sheet for 2 minutes, and then transfer to a cooling rack to cool completely.

Pie fillings: Beat the fondant confectioners' sugar in a bowl with the orange juice and a little orange food coloring to make a smooth frosting that levels when the spoon is lifted from the bowl. If necessary, add a little more orange juice. Spoon a little frosting into the center of each cookie, spreading it into the corners with a toothpick. Sprinkle sparingly with the cocoa powder.

Try me too! page 82

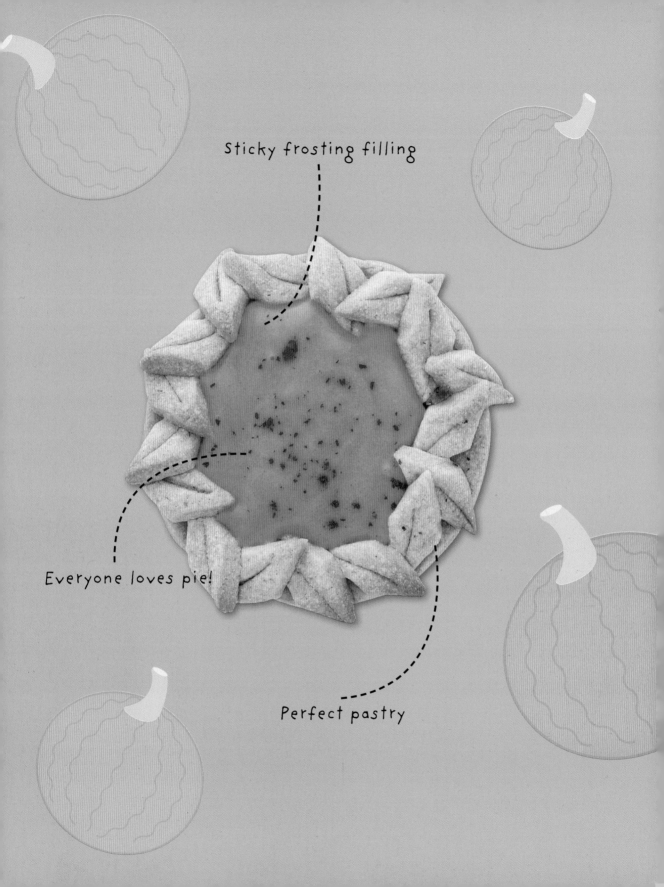

Sticky frosting filling

Everyone loves pie!

Perfect pastry

Trick or Treat Bucket

Ingredients

- 1 quantity lemon cookie dough (see page 7)
- Flour, for dusting
- Orange food coloring
- 1 quantity lemon buttercream (see page 10)
- A small handful of soft licorice pieces
- Selection of small sweets, such as mini marshmallows, jelly beans, and sugar-coated gummy candies

Equipment

- Large cookie sheet
- Rolling pin
- Small sharp knife
- Small spatula
- Parchment paper, for tracing
- Pencil
- Scissors
- Craft knife

Baking: Heat the oven to 375°F (190°C, Gas 6) and grease a large cookie sheet. Roll out the dough on a lightly floured surface until about $1/4$ inch (5 mm) thick and cut out six $2^3/4$-inch (7-cm) squares. Use a sharp knife to taper two opposite sides of each square to create bucket shapes. Place the dough shapes on the cookie sheet, spacing them slightly apart. Gather up the trimmings and reroll to make extra cookies, if liked. Bake in the preheated oven for 12–15 minutes until lightly browned around the edges. Remove from the oven, leave on the cookie sheet for 2 minutes, and then transfer to a cooling rack to cool completely.

Buckets: Beat orange food coloring into the buttercream, adding a little at a time until the desired shade is reached, then spread over the cookies with a small spatula. Trace and cut out the hat and moon templates (see opposite). Roll the licorice out as thinly as possible on a chopping board, and cut around the templates with a craft knife. (Soften the licorice in the microwave for a few seconds if too firm to roll, see page 20.) Repeat to give about 18 hats and 18 moons. Press into the buttercream.

Handles: Cut thin strips, about $3^1/2$ inches (9 cm) long, from more thinly rolled licorice and press into the buttercream to secure in place for handles.

Candies: Position the candies along the tops of the cookies, pressing them into the buttercream to secure.

All hallows' candies

A bucket full
of treats

Delicious licorice

Haunted House

Ingredients

- 1 quantity chocolate cookie dough (see page 7)
- Flour, for dusting
- 5$^1/_2$ oz (150 g) semisweet chocolate, melted (see page 16)
- 12 orange square fruit chews
- 1$^3/_4$ oz (50 g) milk chocolate, melted (see page 16)
- 1 green gummy candy
- Several white square fruit chews

Equipment

- Large cookie sheet
- Parchment, for tracing
- Pencil
- Scissors
- Rolling pin
- Small sharp knife
- 2 paper pastry bags (see page 17)

Baking: Heat the oven to 375°F (190°C, Gas 6). Grease a large cookie sheet, and trace and cut out the haunted house template on page 127. Roll out the dough on a lightly floured surface until about $^1/_4$ inch (5 mm) thick, then cut around the template to shape 6 cookies. Place the dough shapes on the cookie sheet, spacing them slightly apart. Gather up the trimmings and reroll to make extra cookies, if liked. Bake in the preheated oven for 12–15 minutes until lightly browned around the edges. Remove from the oven, leave on the cookie sheet for 2 minutes, and then transfer to a cooling rack to cool completely.

Houses: Put about 2 tablespoons of the melted semisweet chocolate in a paper pastry bag and snip off the merest tip. Use to pipe outlines around the edges of the cookies. Spoon the remaining semisweet chocolate into the outlined areas, spreading the chocolate with the back of a teaspoon. Use a toothpick to spread the chocolate into the corners.

Windows and doors: Trace and cut out the window templates (see opposite). Flatten several of the orange fruit chews until about $^1/_{16}$ inch (2 mm) thick on a chopping board with a rolling pin, and cut around the templates with a craft knife. (Soften the chews in the microwave for a few seconds if too firm to roll, see page 20.) Repeat to give about 16 windows, then press the windows gently onto the chocolate. Put the milk chocolate in a paper pastry bag and snip off the merest tip. Use to pipe window panes and a simple door shape, adding blobs of the semisweet chocolate for door handles. (If the semisweet chocolate has set, melt again very briefly in the microwave, see page 16).

Pumpkins: Soften the remaining fruit chews in the microwave if too firm to mold (see page 16). Break off small pieces and roll into balls. Flatten slightly and impress grooves with the back of a knife to create a pumpkin effect. Position the pumpkins next to the doors. Use a craft knife to cut the green gummy candy into tiny stalk shapes and press into the tops of the pumpkins. Pipe on facial features with milk chocolate.

Ghost: Trace and cut out the ghost template (see opposite). Flatten the white fruit chews on a chopping board with a rolling pin, and cut around the templates with a craft knife. Secure in place, then add eyes using milk chocolate.

Christmas Bauble

Ingredients

- 1 quantity vanilla cookie dough (see page 6)
- Flour, for dusting
- 1 egg white, beaten
- Edible silver decorating dust
- A little vegetable oil, for mixing
- Tube of white decorator frosting
- 36 diamond-shaped gummy candies
- Pearlescent dragées

Equipment

- Large cookie sheet
- Rolling pin
- 3-inch (7.5-cm) round cookie cutter
- Fine paintbrush

Baking: Heat the oven to 375°F (190°C, Gas 6) and grease a large cookie sheet. Roll out the dough on a lightly floured surface until about $^1/_4$ inch (5 mm) thick and cut out 6 cookies using a 3-inch (7.5-cm) round cookie cutter. Place the dough rounds on the cookie sheet, spacing them well apart. Gather up the trimmings and reroll. Cut six $^1/_2$-inch (1-cm) squares from the trimmings, the cut two opposite sides on each so they slope slightly. Brush a little egg white over the widest edge of each dough square, using a fine paintbrush, and position one trimmed square at the top of each round shape. Gently press together to secure. Bake in the preheated oven for 12–15 minutes until lightly browned around the edges. Remove from the oven, leave on the cookie sheet for 5 minutes, and then transfer to a cooling rack to cool completely.

Silver detailing: Wash and dry the paintbrush and use to mix a little silver decorating dust with a dash of vegetable oil. You want a smooth paint-like consistency. Use to paint the tops of the baubles and then 3 curved bands of color across each of the cookies.

Decoration: Pipe lines of white decorator frosting over the edges of the silver bands. Pipe further 2 lines of frosting on each cookie and press into them rows of dragées, as in the picture. Pipe another curved line of frosting across the middle of each cookie and secure a row of diamond-shaped gummy candies. Secure a dragée to the middle of each gummy candy with a dot of frosting.

Try me too! page 42

Deck the halls
with lots of
cookies

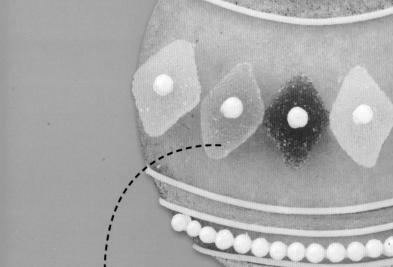

Grinch-proof gummies

Bouncy baubles

What else hangs on Christmas trees...?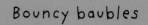

Christmas Star

Ingredients

- 1 quantity ginger cookie dough (see page 7)
- Flour, for dusting
- 1 quantity royal icing (see page 11)
- 9 hard red fruit candies
- Edible red glitter dust

Equipment

- Large cookie sheet
- Parchment paper
- Rolling pin
- 4 and $2^1/_2$-inch (10 and 6-cm) star cookie cutters
- 2 paper pastry bags (see page 17)
- Fine round decorating tip

Baking: Heat the oven to 375°F (190°C, Gas 6). Line a large cookie sheet with parchment paper. Roll out the dough on a lightly floured surface until about $1/_4$ inch (5 mm) thick, then cut out 6 star shapes using a 4-inch (10-cm) star cookie cutter. Place the dough shapes on the cookie sheet, spacing them slightly apart. Using a $2^1/_2$-inch (6-cm) star cookie cutter, cut out the centers of the stars. (Put the centers on the cookie sheet to bake, although they aren't needed to make up this cookie design.) Bake in a preheated oven for 5 minutes.

Red stars: Remove the cookies from the oven and position a candy in the center of each star. Return to the oven for a further 6–8 minutes until lightly browned around the edges and the candies have melted to fill the space. Meanwhile, lightly crush the remaining candies while they still in their wrappers using a rolling pin. Immediately the cookies are removed from the oven, scatter the crushed candy over the melted ones so they're held in place. Leave on the cookie sheet for 5-6 minutes, until the candies are brittle, then transfer to a cooling rack to cool completely.

Decoration: Put a little of the royal icing in a paper pastry bag fitted with a fine round decorating tip. Pipe two outlines near the inner and outer edges of the cookie area of each of the stars. Add a little water to the remaining royal icing to give a thinner consistency (see page 19), then put it in a separate paper pastry bag and snip $1/_4$ inch (5 mm) off the tip. Pipe the icing between the piped lines, spreading it into the corners with a toothpick. Leave to set for about one hour, then pipe a further line of icing along the center of white star on each cookie. Sprinkle a little edible glitter dust over the candy areas. Leave to set completely for several hours or overnight.

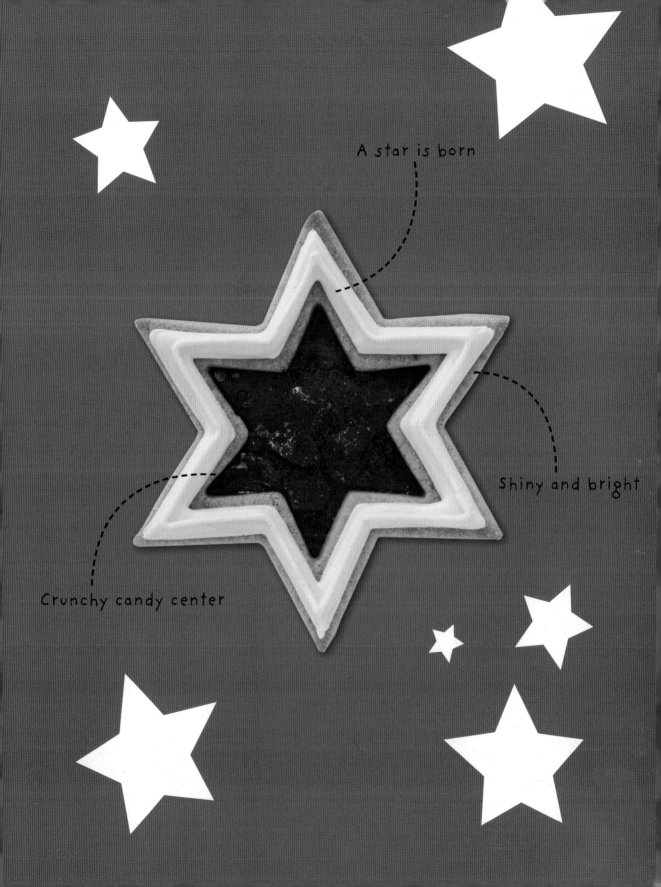

A star is born

Shiny and bright

Crunchy candy center

Christmas Tree

Ingredients

- 1 quantity vanilla cookie dough (see page 6)
- Flour, for dusting
- A small handful of slivered almonds
- White or red gummy candy drops
- Confectioners' sugar, for dusting
- Tube of white and red decorator frosting
- Plenty of red and green candy-coated chocolates
- $2^{1}/_4$ yards (2 metres) red ribbon, about $^{5}/_8$-inch (1.5-cm) thick

Equipment

- Large cookie sheet
- Rolling pin
- 5–inch (13-cm) Christmas tree cookie cutter
- Small star cookie cutter

Baking: Heat the oven to 375°F (190°C, Gas 6) and grease a large cookie sheet. Roll out the dough on a lightly floured surface until about $^{1}/_4$ inch (5 mm) thick and cut out 6 cookies using a 5–inch (13-cm) Christmas tree cookie cutter. Place the dough shapes on the cookie sheet, spacing them slightly apart. Gather up the trimmings and reroll to make extra cookies, if liked. Bake in the preheated oven for 12–15 minutes until lightly browned around the edges. Remove from the oven, leave on the cookie sheet for 2 minutes, and then transfer to a cooling rack to cool completely.

Leaves: Push plenty of slivered almonds into each tree, so they're held in place by the dough. Bake in the preheated oven for 12–15 minutes until lightly browned around the edges. Remove from the oven, leave on the cookie sheet for 2 minutes, and then transfer to a cooling rack to cool completely.

Stars: Flatten the gummy candies with a rolling pin until about 1 inch (2.5 mm) thick, then cut out star shapes with a small star cookie cutter. (Dusting the cutter with confectioners' sugar will make the jellies easier to remove, and if necessary, push a toothpick into the tips of the cutter to help release the candy.) Secure in place over the cookies with decorator frosting, making sure you secure one to the top of each tree. Outline the edges of the stars with white or red decorator frosting.

Finishing touches: Secure the candy-coated chocolates to the trees with dots of decorator frosting. Pipe further white dots in between the sweets. Cut the ribbon into 12-inch (30-cm) lengths and tie around the bases of the trees.

MERRY merry CHRISTMAS!

'Tis the season to eat cookies

Scrummy stars

Oh Christmas tree, Oh Christmas tree

Snowman

Ingredients

- 1 quantity chocolate cookie dough (see page 7)
- Flour, for dusting
- 1 egg white, beaten
- 1 quantity royal icing (see page 11)
- A small handful of currants
- $1^3/_4$ oz (50 g) plain or milk chocolate, melted (see page 16)
- $1^3/_4$ oz (50 g) orange rolled fondant
- Confectioners' sugar, for dusting
- $1^3/_4$ oz (50 g) turquoise rolled fondant

Equipment

- Large cookie sheet
- Rolling pin
- 3-inch and $1^1/_2$-inch (7.5-cm and 4-cm) round cookie cutters
- Small sharp knife
- Fine paintbrush
- 3 paper pastry bags (see page 17)
- Fine round decorating tip
- Scissors
- Small tray
- Parchment paper

Baking: Heat the oven to 375°F (190°C, Gas 6) and grease a large cookie sheet. Roll out the dough on a lightly floured surface until about $^1/_4$ inch (5 mm) thick. Cut out 6 cookies using a 3-inch (7.5-cm) round cookie cutter and 6 cookies using a $1^1/_2$-inch (4-cm) round cookie cutter. Cut a thin slice off one side of each of the rounds, then brush a little egg white over the cut edges. Pair up the small and large rounds on the cookie sheet, pressing them together and spacing each snowman slightly apart. Gather up the trimmings and reroll to make extra cookies, if liked. Bake in the preheated oven for 12–15 minutes until the cookies appear baked but are still slightly soft. Remove from the oven, leave on the cookie sheet for 5 minutes, and then transfer to a cooling rack to cool completely.

Snow and pebbles: Put a little of the royal icing in a paper pastry bag fitted with a fine round decorator tip. Use to pipe outlines around the edges of the cookies, reserving the icing left in the bag. Add a dash of water to the remaining royal icing to give a thinner consistency (see page 19). Put the icing in a separate paper pastry bag and snip $^1/_4$ inch (5 mm) off the tip. Pipe the icing inside the outlined areas of the snowmen, spreading it out with a toothpick. Place currants for eyes and buttons on each cookie, then cut more currants into tiny pieces and arrange for mouths. Leave to set for several hours or overnight.

Arms: Line a small tray with parchment paper. Put the melted chocolate in a pastry bag and snip off the merest tip. Use to pipe at least 12 twig shapes onto the parchment paper. You'll need 2 for each snowman, but it's worth making a few extras in case of breakages. Chill for 30 minutes or until set. Once set, peel away the paper and position the twigs on the cookies, securing with the reserved royal icing from the pastry bag.

Noses: Mold 6 small pieces of orange rolled fondant into carrot shapes and secure in place with royal icing from the pastry bag.

Hats: Shape 6 larger pieces of orange rolled fondant into beanie (bobble) hats, then secure at an angle on the heads. Thinly roll out a small amount of the turquoise fondant and cut into 6 thin strips for the hat trim. Mark vertical lines along each strip with a knife, then secure in place. Roll 6 small pieces of turquoise fondant for bobbles and secure with a dampened paintbrush.

Scarves: Roll out the remaining turquoise and orange fondants. Cut very thin strips of orange fondant and lay them on the turquoise, leaving a gap between each. Roll a rolling pin over the fondants to press the orange into the turquoise. Cut into $5/8$-inch (1.5-cm) wide strips, then into 18 shorter lengths. Make short cuts at one end of 12 of the strips for fringe. Secure a plain strip to each snowman's neck, then secure two fringed strips to each, as in the picture.

Hot Dog

Ingredients

- 1 quantity ginger cookie dough (see page 7)
- Flour, for dusting
- 1 quantity royal icing (see page 11)
- Yellow and brown food coloring
- Sesame seeds
- $2^{1}/_{2}$ oz (75 g) deep red rolled fondant
- Confectioners' sugar, for dusting
- Several green gummy candies

Equipment

- Large cookie sheet
- Parchment paper
- Pencil
- Scissors
- Rolling pin
- 2 paper pastry bags (see page 17)
- Fine round decorating tip
- Toothpick
- Craft knife

Baking: Heat the oven to 375°F (190°C, Gas 6). Grease a large cookie sheet, and trace and cut out the hotdog template on page 124. Roll out the dough on a lightly floured surface until about $^{1}/_{4}$ inch (5 mm) thick, then cut around the template to shape 6 cookies. Place the dough shapes on the cookie sheet, spacing them slightly apart. Gather up the trimmings and reroll to make extra cookies, if liked. Bake in the preheated oven for 12–15 minutes until lightly browned around the edges. Remove from the oven, leave on the cookie sheet for 2 minutes, and then transfer to a cooling rack to cool completely.

Buns: Put 1–2 tablespoons of the royal icing in a paper pastry bag fitted with a fine round decorating tip. Use to pipe outlines around the cookies and then around the sausage shapes. Reserving 3 tablespoons of the remaining royal icing, add a little yellow and brown food coloring to the rest of the icing to resemble the color of bread rolls. Add a little water to give a thinner consistency (see page 19). Put the icing in a separate paper pastry bag and snip $^{1}/_{4}$ inch (5 mm) off the tip. Pipe the icing inside the bread areas of the cookies, spreading it into the corners with a toothpick. Sprinkle with sesame seeds before the icing starts to set.

Lettuce: Thinly roll out the gummy candies on a chopping board with a rolling pin. Cut into jagged pieces using a craft knife, then position the pieces along the top edge of the larger piece of bun on each cookie.

Sausages: Take a $^{1}/_{2}$ oz (15 g) piece of the red rolled fondant and roll it under your hand on a surface lightly dusted with confectioners' sugar to shape a sausage. Position along the center of a cookie, then repeat for the remaining cookies.

Munch! Munch! Munch!

Mustard: Beat yellow food coloring to the reserved 3 tablespoons of royal icing, adding a little at a time until the desired shade is reached, then add a dash of water to give a thinner consistency (see page 19). Put the icing in another paper pastry bag and snip $^1/_4$ inch (5 mm) off the tip. Use to pipe a wiggly line along each of the sausages.

Scrumptious sesame seeds

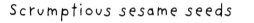

Mmmm mustard

Eat your greens!

Popcorn

Ingredients

- 1 quantity vanilla cookie dough (see page 6)
- Flour, for dusting
- 1 quantity vanilla buttercream (see page 10)
- 5^1/$_2$ oz (150 g) white rolled fondant
- Confectioner's sugar, for dusting
- 2 oz (1^3/$_4$ g) pink rolled fondant
- 2 oz (1^3/$_4$ g) toffee popcorn

Equipment

- Large cookie sheet
- Parchment paper
- Pencil
- Scissors
- Rolling pin
- Small spatula
- Small sharp knife
- Freezer bag
- Fine paintbrush

Baking: Heat the oven to 375°F (190°C, Gas 6). Grease a large cookie sheet, and trace and cut out the popcorn template on page 126. Roll out the dough on a lightly floured surface until about ^{1}/$_4$ inch (5 mm) thick, then cut around the template to shape 6 cookies. Place the dough shapes on the cookie sheet, spacing them slightly apart. Gather up the trimmings and reroll to make extra cookies, if liked. Bake in the preheated oven for 12–15 minutes until lightly browned around the edges. Remove from the oven, leave on the cookie sheet for 2 minutes, and then transfer to a cooling rack to cool completely.

Boxes: Cut out the box area of the template by cutting along the dotted line. Using a small spatula, spread the cookies with the buttercream, leaving an ^{1}/$_2$-inch (1-cm) edge at the bottom and on the two sides. Spread the buttercream more thickly along the top of the cookies where the popcorn will be. Roll out the white rolled fondant on a surface dusted with confectioners' sugar until about ^{1}/$_{16}$ inch (2 mm) thick. Place the template on the fondant, cut around to shape the box, and position the over the buttercream, pressing down gently around the edges. Repeat for the remaining cookies. Roll out the pink fondant and cut into thin strips. You will need about 56. Lay 9 strips on the white fondant on each cookie, as in the picture, pressing the pink fondant down gently and trimming off any excess at the top and bottom of the box shape.

Popcorn: Put the popcorn in a freezer bag and lightly crush the popcorn into smaller pieces with a rolling pin. Arrange on the buttercream at the top of each cookie, pressing the pieces down gently to secure. Put additional pieces of popcorn over the first layer, securing in place with buttercream scrapings left in the bowl.

Popping delicious

Labels: Thinly roll out the white fondant trimmings and cut out small oval shapes, each measuring about $3/4$ x $1/2$ inches (2 x 1.5 cm). Secure to the fronts of the boxes with a dampened paintbrush.

Super stripes

Popcorn

Teapot

Ingredients

- 1 quantity ginger cookie dough (see page 7)
- Flour, for dusting
- $1^3/_4$ oz (50 g) white rolled fondant
- Confectioners' sugar, for dusting
- Tubes of white and red decorator frosting
- 24 red heart-shaped sugar-coated candies

Equipment

- Large cookie sheet
- Parchment paper, for tracing
- Pencil
- Scissors
- Rolling pin
- Small sharp knife

Baking: Heat the oven to 375°F (190°C, Gas 6). Grease a large cookie sheet, and trace and cut out the teapot template on page 123. Roll out the dough on a lightly floured surface until about $1/_4$ inch (5 mm) thick, then cut around the template to shape 6 cookies. Place the dough shapes on the cookie sheet, spacing them slightly apart. Gather up the trimmings and reroll to make extra cookies, if liked. Bake in the preheated oven for 12–15 minutes until lightly browned around the edges. Remove from the oven, leave on the cookie sheet for 2 minutes, and then transfer to a cooling rack to cool completely.

Teapots: Roll out the white rolled fondant on a surface dusted with confectioners' sugar until about $1/_{16}$ inch (2 mm) thick. Cut out $2^3/_4$ x 1-inch (7 x 2.5-cm) rectangles. Pipe a little white decorator frosting across the centers of the teapot shapes and secure the rectangles in place, curving them slightly to fit. Use the white and red decorator frosting to pipe the outlines and lids of the teapots, as in the picture.

Decoration: Secure in place on each cookie the heart-shaped candies along the middle panel and as lid handles with decorator frosting. Pipe dots of red decorator frosting between the hearts along the middle panel.

Try me too! page 92

Wedding Cake

Ingredients

- 1 quantity lemon cookie dough (see page 7)
- Flour, for dusting
- 1 egg white, beaten
- 1 quantity royal icing (see page 11)
- Lemon juice, for thinning
- 1³/₄ oz (50 g) white rolled fondant
- Confectioners' sugar, for dusting

Equipment

- Large cookie sheet
- Rolling pin
- Small sharp knife
- Fine paintbrush
- Paper pastry bag (see page 17)
- Fine round decorating tip
- Toothpick
- ³/₈ and ¹/₂-inch (8-mm and 1-cm) flower plunger or cookie cutters

Baking: Heat the oven to 375°F (190°C, Gas 6) and grease a large cookie sheet. Roll out the dough on a lightly floured surface until about ¹/₄ inch (5 mm) thick. Cut out six 2³/₄ x 1¹/₄-inch (7 x 3-cm) rectangles, six 2 x ³/₄-inch (5 x 3-cm) rectangles and six 1¹/₄-inch (3-cm) squares. Arrange the shapes in stacks of three on the cookie sheet, brushing a little egg white over the edges to be joined using a fine paintbrush, and pushing them firmly together. Gather up the trimmings and reroll to make extra cookies, if liked. Bake in the preheated oven for 12–15 minutes until lightly browned around the edges. Remove from the oven, leave on the cookie sheet for 5 minutes, and then transfer to a cooling rack to cool completely.

White fondant: Put a little of the royal icing in a paper pastry bag fitted with a fine round decorator tip. Use to pipe outlines around the edges of the cookies, reserving the icing left in the bag. Add a little lemon juice to the remaining royal icing to give a thinner consistency (see page 19). Put the icing in a paper pastry bag and snip ¹/₄ inch (5mm) off the tip. Pipe the icing inside the outlined areas of the cakes, spreading it out with a toothpick. Leave to set for several hours or overnight.

Decoration: Use the reserved royal icing in the bag to pipe scallop shapes (see page 19) along the top of each tier. Roll out the white rolled fondant on a surface dusted with confectioners' sugar until about ¹/₁₆ inch (2 mm) thick, and moisten the top of each tier on the cookies with a dampened paintbrush. Cut out lots of flower shapes using ³/₈-inch and ¹/₂-inch (8-mm and 1-cm) flower cutters, positioning the flowers on the cookies as they are cut. Pipe dots of the reserved royal icing into the centers of the flowers.

Congratulations!

I now pronounce
you totally delicious

Here comes
the cookie

Ice Cream Cone

Ingredients

- 1 quantity vanilla cookie dough (see page 6)
- Flour, for dusting
- 1³/₄ oz (50 g) milk or semisweet chocolate, melted (see page 16)
- 3¹/₂ oz (100 g) confectioners' sugar
- ¹/₂ teaspoon vanilla extract or bean paste
- Yellow food coloring
- Multicolored candy sprinkles

Equipment

- Large cookie sheet
- Parchment paper, for tracing
- Pencil
- Scissor
- Rolling pin
- Small sharp knife
- Paper pastry bag (see page 17)

Baking: Heat the oven to 375°F (190°C, Gas 6). Grease a large cookie sheet, and trace and cut out the ice cream template on page 124. Roll out the dough on a lightly floured surface until about ¹/₄ inch (5 mm) thick, then cut around the template to shape 6 cookies. Using the back of a knife, make shallow grooves about ¹/₂ inch (1 cm) apart diagonally across the cone area, first in one direction and then the opposite direction. Place the dough shapes on the cookie sheet, spacing them slightly apart. Gather up the trimmings and reroll to make extra cookies, if liked. Bake in the preheated oven for 12–15 minutes until lightly browned around the edges. Remove from the oven, leave on the cookie sheet for 2 minutes, and then transfer to a cooling rack to cool completely.

Chocolate sticks: Put the melted chocolate in a paper pastry bag and snip ¹/₄ inch (5 mm) off the tip. Line a tray with parchment paper and scribble lines back and forth to cover an area of about 1¹/₂ x ⁵/₈ inches (4 x 1.5 cm). You'll need 6 chocolate sticks, but it's worth making a few extras in case of breakages. Leave to set for several hours or overnight.

Ice cream: Beat the confectioners' sugar in a bowl with the vanilla, a dash of yellow food coloring, and about 1 tablespoon water to make a paste that thickly coats the back of a teaspoon. Spoon the frosting over the tops of the cookies so that it coats them in a smooth but thick layer. (If the icing is too thin, add a little more confectioners' sugar, and if it's too thick a drop more water). Scatter candy sprinkles over the frosting. Carefully lift the chocolate sticks from the paper and rest them at an angle on the icing.

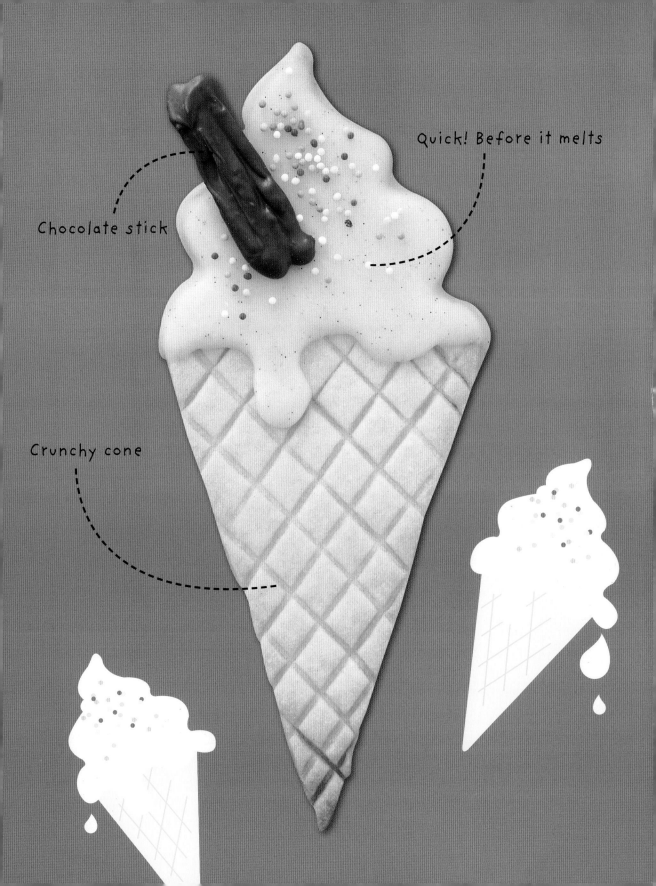

Chocolate stick

Quick! Before it melts

Crunchy cone

Strawberry

Ingredients

- 1 quantity vanilla cookie dough (see page 6)
- Flour, for dusting
- 1 quantity royal icing (see page 11)
- Red food coloring
- 1 oz (25 g) green rolled fondant
- Confectioners' sugar, for dusting

Equipment

- Large cookie sheet
- Rolling pin
- 3$\frac{1}{4}$-inch (8-cm) heart cookie cutter
- 2 paper pastry bags (see page 17)
- Fine round decorating tip
- Toothpick
- $\frac{3}{8}$-inch (8-mm) star cookie cutter

Baking: Preheat the oven to 375°F (190°C, Gas 6) and grease a large cookie sheet. Roll out the dough on a lightly floured surface until about $\frac{1}{4}$ inch (5 mm) thick and cut out 6 cookies using a 3$\frac{1}{4}$-inch (8-cm) heart cookie cutter. Place the dough rounds on the cookie sheet, spacing them slightly apart. Gather up the trimmings and reroll to make extra cookies, if liked. Bake in the preheated oven for 12–15 minutes until lightly browned around the edges. Remove from the oven, leave on the cookie sheet for 2 minutes, and then transfer to a cooling rack to cool completely.

Strawberries: Put 1–2 tablespoons of the royal icing in a paper pastry bag fitted with a fine round decorating tip. Use to pipe outlines around the edges of the cookies, reserving the icing left in the bag. Beat red food coloring into the remaining royal icing, adding a little at a time until the desired shade is reached, then add a dash of water to give a thinner consistency (see page 19). Put the icing in a separate paper pastry bag and snip $\frac{1}{4}$ inch (5 mm) off the tip. Pipe the icing inside the outlined areas of the strawberries, spreading it out with a toothpick. Leave to set for several hours or overnight.

Seeds: On each of the strawberries, pipe tiny dots of white royal icing, trailing the icing away as you release the pressure to create seed shapes (see page 19).

Try me too! page 56

Stalks: Thinly roll out the green rolled fondant on a surface dusted with confectioners' sugar. Cut out 6 star shapes with a $3/8$-inch (8-mm) star cookie cutter. Pipe a dot of white royal icing at the top of each strawberry. Pinch the points of the stars slightly so they resemble the points of a stalk and press the stalks in place on the cookies. From the fondant trimming, mold short lengths, about $1/2$ inch (1 cm) long. Press into the centers of the stalk shapes.

Fondant stalk

Fun fruit cookie

Strawberries and cream anyone?

Gingerbread House

Ingredients

- 1 quantity ginger cookie dough (see page 7)
- Flour, for dusting
- 6 red or pink hard fruit candies
- 6 pale pink square fruit chews
- 2 tubes of white decorator frosting
- A small handful of small pink, yellow, and red jelly beans
- 12 deep pink square fruit chews

Equipment

- Large cookie sheet
- Baking parchment
- Pencil
- Scissors
- Rolling pin
- Small sharp knife
- $^3/_4$-inch (2-cm) heart cookie cutter
- Craft knife

Baking: Heat the oven to 375°F (190°C, Gas 6). Grease a large cookie sheet, and trace and cut out the gingerbread house template on page 123. Roll out the dough on a lightly floured surface until about $^1/_4$ inch (5 mm) thick, then cut around the template to shape 6 cookies. Place the dough shapes on the cookie sheet, spacing them slightly apart. Gather up the trimmings and reroll to make extra cookies, if liked. Using a $^3/_4$-inch (2-cm) heart cookie cutter, cut out 2 shapes on each cookie for windows. Bake in a preheated oven for 5 minutes.

Windows: While the cookies are baking, lightly crush the hard candy while they still in their wrappers using a rolling pin. Remove the cookies from the oven and position a few pieces of crushed candy in each of the window holes. Return to the oven for a further 7–10 minutes until the cookies are lightly browned around the edges and the candies have melted. Leave on the cookie sheet for 5–6 minutes until the sweets are brittle, then transfer to a cooling rack to cool completely.

Doors: Trace and cut out the door template (see opposite). Flatten the pale pink fruit chews with a rolling pin on a chopping board. (Soften the chews in the microwave for a few seconds if too firm to mold, see page 20.) Cut around the template with a craft knife to shape the 6 doors. Secure in place with a little white decorator frosting.

Beware the witch! -----

Snow: Pipe snow onto each roof and chimney using the white decorator frosting, then add vertical lines of piping for icicles.

Finishing touches: Cut the jelly beans in half and use to decorate each roof. Pipe a line of decorating frosting down the sides of each house. Cut the deep pink chews into dice and secure a row down each side. Pipe window frames, and door frames and handles with white decorating frosting.

Sugary snow

Candy windows

Teddy Bear

Ingredients

- 1 quantity ginger cookie dough (see page 7)
- Flour, for dusting
- $3^{1}/_{2}$ oz (100 g) green rolled fondant
- Confectioners' sugar, for dusting
- 1 quantity vanilla buttercream
- $1^{3}/_{4}$ oz (50 g) pink rolled fondant
- $1^{3}/_{4}$ oz (50 g) lilac rolled fondant
- Small piece each of red and white rolled fondant
- Blue and brown food coloring

Equipment

- Large cookie sheet
- Rolling pin
- $4^{1}/_{4}$–$4^{1}/_{2}$-inch (11–12-cm) teddy bear cookie cutter
- Parchment paper
- Pencil
- Scissors
- 3 and $1^{1}/_{4}$-inch (7.5 and 3-cm) round cookie cutters
- Small spatula
- Toothpick
- Fine paintbrush
- Small flower plunger or cookie cutter

Baking: Heat the oven to 375°F (190°C, Gas 6) and grease a large cookie sheet. Roll out the dough on a lightly floured surface until about $^{1}/_{4}$ inch (5 mm) thick and cut out 6 cookies using a teddy cookie cutter, about $4^{1}/_{4}$–$4^{1}/_{2}$-inches (11–12-cm) long. Place the dough shapes on the cookie sheet, spacing them slightly apart. Gather up the trimmings and reroll to make extra cookies, if liked. Bake in the preheated oven for 12–15 minutes until lightly browned around the edges. Remove from the oven, leave on the cookie sheet for 2 minutes, and then transfer to a cooling rack to cool completely.

T-Shirts: Using the teddy bear cookie cutter as a guide for size and outline, design a T-shirt template similar to the picture, if liked, on parchment paper and cut out. Roll out the green fondant on a surface dusted with confectioners' sugar until about $^{1}/_{16}$ inch (2 mm) thick, and cut around the template. Repeat to give 6 T-shirts. Spread a little buttercream over the underside of the T-shirts and secure in place.

Skirts: Roll out the pink fondant until about $^{1}/_{16}$ inch (2 mm) thick and cut out three 3-inch (7.5 cm) rounds using a cookie cutter. Cut out the centers using an $1^{1}/_{4}$-inch (3-cm) cookie cutter, then cut the rings in half. Roll a toothpick around the outer edge of each semicircle so that it starts to frill (see page 14). Repeat with the rolled green fondant trimmings and the lilac fondant to give 6 frills in each color.

Spread a little buttercream over the skirt areas of the cookies. Lay a pink fondant frilled semi-circle across each teddy for the bottom skirt frill, then attach two more layers of frill in green and lilac, each position about $^{1}/_{4}$ inch (5 mm) above the previous frill. Using the tip of a toothpick, lift up the frilled edges to open them out.

Faces: Shape and position tiny balls of white fondant for the eyes and red fondant for lips, securing with dots of buttercream. Using a fine paintbrush, paint the centers of the eyes with blue food coloring. Paint noses and eyebrows onto the cookies using brown food coloring.

Finishing touches: Use the pink fondant trimmings to shape 3 tiny buttons on each cookie, securing in place with a dampened paintbrush. Make buttonholes with the end of a toothpick. Use a small flower plunger or cookie cutter to shape 6 small pink fondant flowers and secure in place with buttercream. Mold 6 tiny balls of pink fondant and secure at the center of each flower with a dampened paintbrush.

Pretty frilly skirt

Princess' Crown

Ingredients

- 1 quantity vanilla cookie dough (see page 6)
- Flour, for dusting
- 1 quantity royal icing (see page 11)
- Pink food coloring
- Pastel colored candy sprinkles
- Silver dragées, in several sizes
- Small pink candy-coated chocolates
- Several small yellow or pink gummy candies

Equipment

- Large cookie sheet
- Rolling pin
- Small sharp knife
- 2 paper pastry bags (see page 17)
- Fine round decorating tip
- Scissors
- Toothpick
- Craft knife

Baking: Heat the oven to 375°F (190°C, Gas 6) and grease a large cookie sheet. Roll out the dough on a lightly floured surface until about $1/4$ inch (5 mm) thick and cut out six 4 x 2-inch (10 x 5-cm) rectangles. Cut 4 deep notches along one short end of each rectangle. Place the dough shapes on the cookie sheet, spacing them well apart, and open out the points slightly so they resemble crown shapes Gather up the trimmings and reroll to make extra cookies, if liked. Bake in the preheated oven for 12–15 minutes until lightly browned around the edges. Remove from the oven, leave on the cookie sheet for 2 minutes, and then transfer to a cooling rack to cool completely.

Crowns: Put about 2 tablespoons of the royal icing in a paper pastry bag fitted with a fine round decorator tip. Use to pipe outlines around the edges of the cookies, reserving the icing left in the bag. Add a dash of water to the remaining royal icing to give a thinner consistency (see page 19). Beat in a little pink food coloring. Put the icing in a separate paper pastry bag and snip $1/4$ inch (5 mm) off the tip. Pipe the icing inside the outlined areas of the crowns, spreading it out with a toothpick.

Jewels: While the royal icing is still soft, scatter candy sprinkles and silver dragées over the icing. Leave to set for several hours or overnight.

Finishing touches: Pipe a dot of reserved royal icing from the pastry bag at the points of the crowns and secure a mini candy-coated chocolate and silver ball to each point. Scribble plenty more icing along the base of the crowns in a thick, raised band. Thinly slice the gummy candies using a craft knife and cut into diamond shapes. Arrange over the white icing.

I crown you queen
of the cookies

Perfect
princess
piping

Shiny sprinkles

Guess how the princess gets about...

Kiddie's Car

Ingredients

- 1 quantity chocolate cookie dough (see page 7)
- Flour, for dusting
- Tubes of white and black decorator frosting
- 1 quantity royal icing (see page 11)
- Red food coloring
- 12 silver heart dragées
- 12 square yellow sugar-coated candies
- 12 small blue candy-coated chocolate

Equipment

- Large cookie sheet
- Rolling pin
- Parchment paper, for tracing
- Pencil
- Scissors
- Small sharp knife
- Paper pastry bag
- Toothpick

Baking: Heat the oven to 375°F (190°C, Gas 6). Grease a large cookie sheet, and trace and cut out the car template on page 122. Roll out the dough on a lightly floured surface until about $1/4$ inch (5 mm) thick, then cut around the template to shape 6 cookies. Place the dough shapes on the cookie sheet, spacing them slightly apart. Gather up the trimmings and reroll to make extra cookies, if liked. Bake in the preheated oven for 12–15 minutes until the cookies appear baked but are still slightly soft. Remove from the oven, leave on the cookie sheet for 2 minutes, and then transfer to a cooling rack to cool completely.

Bodywork: Use the white decorator frosting to pipe outlines around the edges of the cookies and window areas. Beat red food coloring into the royal icing, adding a little at a time until the desired shade is reached, then add a little water to give a thinner consistency (see page 19). Put the icing in a paper pastry bag and snip $1/4$ inch (5 mm) off the tip. Pipe the icing inside the outlined areas of the car, spreading it out with a toothpick. Leave to set for several hours or overnight.

Lights and radiators: Use white decorator frosting to pipe a radiator, resemble smiling mouths, onto each of the cookies. Secure a silver heart dragée on either side of each radiator with a little decorating frosting.

Wheels: Use black decorator frosting to pipe the outlines of the wheels, then fill in with more piping.

Brum! BRUM!
Bruuummmm!

Finishing touches: Use black decorator frosting to pipe sun visors on the window areas of the cookies. Secure the yellow candies for eyes, adding white centers of decorator frosting, and then the blue candies to finish.

Eyes on the road!

Yummy crunchy lights

Full speed ahead

Spaceship

Ingredients

- 1 quantity chocolate cookie dough (see page 7)
- Flour, for dusting
- 1³/₄ oz (50 g) white chocolate, melted (see page 16)
- 7 oz (200 g) blue rolled fondant
- Confectioners' sugar, for dusting
- 2–3 lengths of sugar-coated red chewy fruit roll
- 1³/₄ oz (50 g) white rolled fondant
- Tubes of red and yellow decorator frosting
- Black food coloring
- Several pink square fruit chews

Equipment

- Large cookie sheet
- Rolling pin
- Parchment paper, for tracing
- Pencil
- Scissors
- Craft knife
- Paper pastry bag (see page 17)
- 1³/₄-inch and 1¹/₄-inch (4.5-cm and 3-cm) round cookie cutters
- Fine paintbrush

Baking: Heat the oven to 375°F (190°C, Gas 6). Grease a large cookie sheet, and trace and cut out the spaceship template on page 123. Roll out the dough on a lightly floured surface until about ¹/₄ inch (5 mm) thick, then cut around the template to shape 6 cookies. Place the dough shapes on the cookie sheet, spacing them slightly apart. Gather up the trimmings and reroll to make extra cookies, if liked. Bake in the preheated oven for 12–15 minutes until lightly browned around the edges. Remove from the oven, leave on the cookie sheet for 2 minutes, and then transfer to a cooling rack to cool completely.

Spaceship: Put the melted white chocolate in a paper pastry bag and snip off the merest tip. Roll out the blue rolled fondant on a surface dusted with confectioners' sugar until about ¹/₁₆ inch (2 mm) thick. Cut the fins off the spaceship template and reserve, then cut around the template to shape the rockets. Cut a circle out of the center of the fondant shapes using a 1³/₄-inch (4.5-cm) round cookie cutter. Pipe a little chocolate over the underside of the blue fondant and secure in place. Place the fin parts of the template over the chewy fruit roll and cut around with scissors to give 12 fins. Cut the front tip off the template and cut 6 front tips from the chewy fruit roll. Secure in place with melted chocolate.

Spacemen: Roll out the white rolled fondant on a surface dusted with confectioners' sugar until about ¹/₁₆ inch (2 mm) thick, then cut out circles using a 1¹/₄-inch (3-cm) round cookie cutter. Cut out squares from the fondant rounds to shape spaceman helmets and secure in place with melted chocolate. Using the white fondant trimmings, roll tiny balls of fondant between your finger and thumb for eyes and secure in place.

Up, up and away

Smiley spaceman

Use the red decorator frosting to pipe noses, mouths and detail on the helmets, and the yellow decorator frosting to pipe the hair. Paint the centers of the eyes using a fine paintbrush and black food coloring. Soften the pale pink fruit chews very briefly in the microwave for a few seconds if very firm (see page 20), then take pea-sized pieces and shape into 6 tiny hands. Secure in place.

Finishing touches: Use red decorator frosting to pipe details at the tail end of the rockets. Use the white chocolate to pipe decorative trim around the edges of the rockets. (Soften the pastry bag of white chocolate very briefly in the microwave if it has started to set, see page 16.)

whooosh!
WHOOSH!

Eyeball

Ingredients

- 1 quantity ginger cookie dough (see page 7)
- Flour, for dusting
- 1 quantity royal icing (see page 11)
- Blue and red food coloring
- 1¹/₂ oz (40 g) white rolled fondant
- Confectioners' sugar, for dusting
- 6 brown candy-coated chocolates

Equipment

- Large cookie sheet
- Rolling pin
- 3-inch (7.5-cm) round cookie cutter
- Paper pastry bag (see page 17)
- Fine round decorating tip
- Fine paintbrush

Baking: Heat the oven to 375°F (190°C, Gas 6) and grease a large cookie sheet. Roll out the dough on a lightly floured surface until about ¹/₄ inch (5 mm) thick and cut out 6 cookies using a 3-inch (7.5-cm) round cookie cutter. Place the dough rounds on the cookie sheet, spacing them slightly apart. Gather up the trimmings and reroll to make extra cookies, if liked. Bake in the preheated oven for 12–15 minutes until lightly browned around the edges. Remove from the oven, leave on the cookie sheet for 2 minutes, and then transfer to a cooling rack to cool completely.

Whites: Put 1–2 tablespoons of the royal icing in a paper pastry bag fitted with a fine round decorating tip. Use to pipe outlines around the edges of the cookies, leaving a slight gap between the icing and the edge. Add a dash of water to the remaining icing to give a thinner consistency (see page 19). Spoon the icing into the outlined areas, spreading it to the piped lines with the back of a teaspoon. Leave to set for several hours or overnight.

Pupils: Knead a little blue food coloring into the white rolled fondant until it's still slightly unevenly mixed. Take 6 grape-sized pieces, roll into small balls on a surface lightly dusted with confectioners' sugar, and then flatten. Place the flattened pieces of blue fondant in the middle of the cookies, then position a sugar-coated candy at the center of blue fondant, securing in place with a dampened paintbrush.

Bloodshot markings: Dilute a little red food coloring in a few drops of water. Using a fine paintbrush, add "bloodshot" markings over the white sections of the cookies.

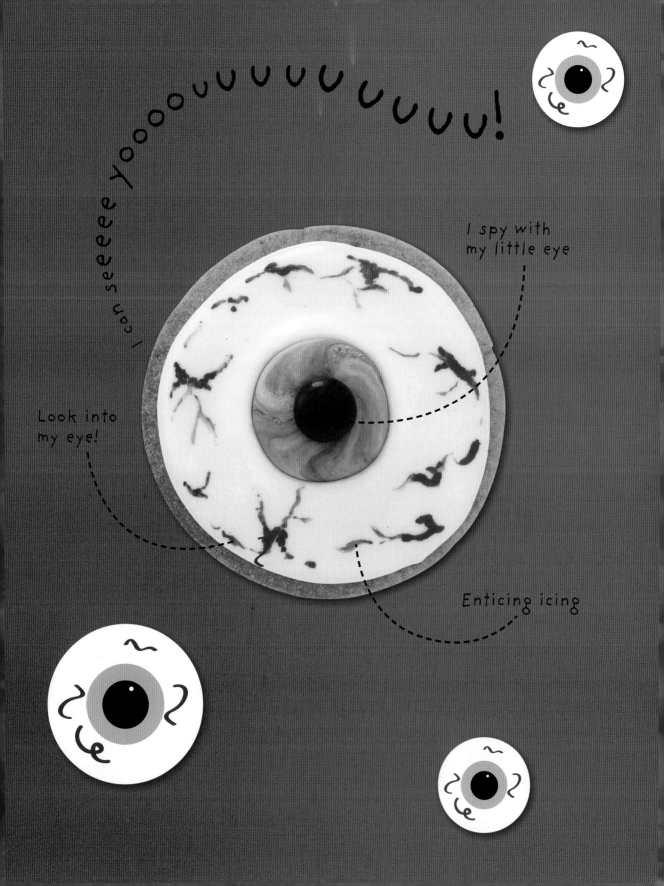

I can seeee yoooouuuuuuuuuuuu!

I spy with
my little eye

Look into
my eye!

Enticing icing

Sun

Ingredients

- 1 quantity chocolate cookie dough (see page 7)
- Flour, for dusting
- 1 egg white, beaten
- Tubes of white and red decorator frosting
- Yellow, blue, brown, and red food coloring
- 1 quantity royal icing (see page 11)
- Several white fruit chews
- 1 sugar-coated red chewy fruit roll
- 6 pieces soft licorice

Equipment

- Large cookie sheet
- Rolling pin
- 3-inch (7.5-cm) round cookie cutter
- Small sharp knife
- Fine paintbrush
- Paper pastry bag (see page 17)
- Toothpick
- Parchment paper, for tracing
- Pencil
- Scissors
- Craft knife

Baking: Heat the oven to 375°F (190°C, Gas 6) and grease a large cookie sheet. Roll out the dough on a lightly floured surface until about $1/4$ inch (5 mm) thick and cut out 6 cookies using a 3-inch (7.5-cm) round cookie cutter. Place the dough rounds on the cookie sheet, spacing them well apart. Gather up the trimmings, reroll, and cut into $3/4$-inch (2-cm) strips. Make diagonal cuts across the strips to make triangular shapes. Brush the edges of the cookie rounds with beaten egg white using a fine paintbrush, then press the triangles around the cookies, pushing them firmly in place. Bake in the preheated oven for 12–15 minutes until the cookies appear baked but are still slightly soft. Remove from the oven, leave on the cookie sheet for 5 minutes, and then transfer to a cooling rack to cool completely.

Suns: Use the white decorator frosting to pipe outlines around the edges of the cookies. Beat yellow food coloring into the royal icing, adding a little at a time until the desired shade is reached, then add a little water to give a thinner consistency (see page 19). Put the icing in a paper pastry bag and snip $1/4$ inch (5 mm) off the tip. Pipe the icing inside the outlined areas of the suns, spreading it out with a toothpick. Leave to set for several hours or overnight.

Features: Trace and cut out the eye templates (see opposite). Soften the white fruit chews very briefly in the microwave for a few seconds if firm (see page 20). Place the chews on a chopping board and cut out 6 sets of eyes using a craft knife. Position the eyes on the cookies. Tear off 6 pieces of red chewy fruit roll, shape into smiling mouths, and secure in place. Using a fine paintbrush, paint the centers of the eyes with blue food coloring, then add eyebrows using brown food color and mouth details using red food color, as in the picture. Pipe white decorator frosting around the eyes.

Hats: Trace and cut out the hat template (see right). Flatten the licorice pieces with a rolling pin, softening them briefly in the microwave if too firm, and cut out hats using a craft knife. Secure in place with a little decorator frosting.

The sun has got his hat on!

I'm walking on sunshine

Bikini

Ingredients

- 1 quantity lemon cookie dough (see page 7)
- Flour, for dusting
- Black and yellow food coloring
- 1 quantity royal icing (see page 11)
- Lemon juice, for thinning
- Small piece of white rolled fondant
- Confectioners' sugar, for dusting

Equipment

- Large cookie sheet
- Parchment paper, for tracing
- Pencil
- Scissors
- Rolling pin
- Small sharp knife
- 2 paper pastry bags (see page 17)
- Fine round decorating tip
- Toothpick
- $^3/_8$-inch (8-mm) flower plunger or cookie cutter

Baking: Heat the oven to 375°F (190°C, Gas 6). Grease a large cookie sheet, and trace and cut out the bikini template on page 126. Roll out the dough on a lightly floured surface until about $^1/_4$ inch (5 mm) thick, then cut around the template to shape 6 cookie bikini sets. Place the dough shapes on the cookie sheet, spacing them slightly apart. Gather up the trimmings and reroll to make extra cookies, if liked. Bake in the preheated oven for 12–15 minutes until lightly browned around the edges. Remove from the oven, leave on the cookie sheet for 2 minutes, and then transfer to a cooling rack to cool completely.

Bikinis: Add black food coloring to one-third of the royal icing and put in a paper pastry bag fitted with a fine round decorating tip. Use to pipe outlines around the edges of the bikini shapes. Beat yellow food coloring into the remaining royal icing, adding a little at a time until the desired shade is reached, then add a few drops of lemon juice to give a thinner consistency (see page 19). Put the icing in a second paper pastry bag and snip $^1/_4$ inch (5 mm) off the tip. Pipe the icing inside the outlined areas of the bikini pieces, spreading it out with a toothpick. While the icing is still soft, pipe dots of black royal icing onto the yellow icing. Leave to set for several hours or overnight.

Flowers: Roll out the white rolled fondant on a surface dusted with confectioners' sugar until about $^1/_{16}$ inch (2 mm) thick, then cut out 12 tiny flower shapes. Secure each flower in place with a dot of royal icing. Pipe a dot of black royal icing into the center of each flower.

Teeny weeny yellow polka dot bikini

Silky royal icing

It's beach time!

These would look good with... ☞

Designer Shopping Bag

Ingredients

- 1 quantity lemon cookie dough (see page 7)
- Flour, for dusting
- 6 pale pink square fruit chews
- 1 quantity lemon buttercream (see page 10)
- 7 oz (200 g) white rolled fondant
- Confectioners' sugar, for dusting
- 18 mini pink marshmallows
- 6 mini candy-coated chocolates
- 2$\frac{1}{4}$ yards (2 metres) pink or brown ribbon, up to $\frac{1}{2}$-inch (1-cm) wide

Equipment

- Large cookie sheet
- Rolling pin
- Small sharp knife
- Large skewer or fine paintbrush
- Scissors
- Small spatula
- Paper pastry bag (see page 17)

Baking: Heat the oven to 375°F (190°C, Gas 6) and grease a large cookie sheet. Roll out the dough on a lightly floured surface until about $\frac{1}{4}$ inch (5 mm) thick and cut out six 3$\frac{1}{2}$ x 2$\frac{3}{4}$-inch (9 x 7-cm) rectangles. Place the dough shapes on the cookie sheet, spacing them slightly apart. Using a large skewer or the handle end of a fine paintbrush, make 2 holes about $\frac{1}{2}$ inch (1 cm) in from one short edge on each of the rectangles. Gather up the trimmings and reroll to make extra cookies, if liked. Bake in the preheated oven for 12–15 minutes until lightly browned around the edges. Remove from the oven and immediately remake the handle holes, as they may have closed up a little during baking. Leave the cookies on the cookie sheet for 2 minutes, and then transfer to a cooling rack to cool completely.

Tissue paper: Soften the pale pink fruit chews very briefly in the microwave for a few seconds if very firm (see page 20). Flatten until about $\frac{1}{16}$-inch (2-mm) thick with a rolling pin, then cut each chew into jagged pieces with scissors. Using a small spatula, spread a little buttercream along the top edge of the cookies (above the handle holes) and secure the pieces of chew over the buttercream.

Bags: Spread more buttercream over the cookies, leaving a $\frac{1}{2}$-inch (1-cm) edge. Roll out the white rolled fondant on a surface dusted with confectioners' sugar until about $\frac{1}{16}$ inch (2 mm) thick. Cut out six 3$\frac{1}{4}$ x 2$\frac{1}{2}$-inch (8 x 6-cm) rectangles and secure to the cookies, pressing them down gently around the edges. Hold each cookie up to the light, so you can see the holes in the cookies,

Spotty ribbon

Magnificent marshmallow

and push the skewer or handle end of the paintbrush through the fondant to make holes in the fondant.

Flowers: Put the remaining buttercream in a paper pastry bag and snip off the merest tip. Cut the marshmallows in half lengthways. Secure the candy-coated chocolates and marshmallow pieces to the fronts of the bags using buttercream from the pastry bag, as in the picture.

Handles: Cut the ribbon into 6 lengths and thread through the holes. Tie knots at the back to secure, and trim off the excess ribbon.

Platform Shoes

Ingredients

- 1 quantity vanilla cookie dough (see page 6)
- Flour, for dusting
- 1 quantity royal icing (see page 11)
- Orange, red, and pink food coloring
- 6 pink or orange square sugar-coated fruit candies

Equipment

- Large cookie sheet
- Parchment paper, for tracing
- Pencil
- Scissors
- Small sharp knife
- Rolling pin
- 4 paper pastry bags (see page 17)
- Fine round decorating tip
- Toothpick

Baking: Heat the oven to 375°F (190°C, Gas 6). Grease a large cookie sheet, and trace and cut out the shoe template on page 125. Roll out the dough on a lightly floured surface until about $^1/_4$ inch (5 mm) thick, then cut around the template to shape 6 cookies. Place the dough shapes on the cookie sheet, spacing them slightly apart. Gather up the trimmings and reroll to make extra cookies, if liked. Bake in the preheated oven for 12–15 minutes until lightly browned around the edges. Remove from the oven, leave on the cookie sheet for 2 minutes, and then transfer to a cooling rack to cool completely.

Bases: Beat orange food coloring into one-third of the buttercream, adding a little at a time until the desired shade is reached, then put in a paper pastry bag fitted with a fine round decorating tip. Use to pipe outlines around the edges of the cookies. Also pipe a line between the strap and the shoe, across the top of the heel, and between the shoe and the platform and sole areas, to identify and keep the different parts of the shoe separate.

Shoes: Beat red food coloring into two-thirds of the remaining royal icing, adding a little at a time until the desired shade is reached, then add a dash of water to give a thinner consistency (see page 19). Put the icing in a separate paper pastry bag and snip $^1/_4$ inch (5 mm) off the tip. Pipe the icing inside the outlined shoe and sole areas, spreading it out with a toothpick.

Heels and platforms: Color half the remaining icing with orange food coloring and half with pink, adding a little at a time until the desired shade. Thin each with a dash of water to give the same thinner consistency, put in separate pastry bags and snip off the merest tips. Use to fill in the heel, platform, and strap areas.

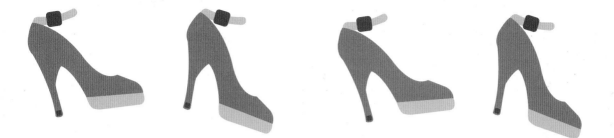

Buckles: Secure the pink or orange sugar-coated candies to the straps using royal icing from one of the bags. Leave to set for several hours or overnight.

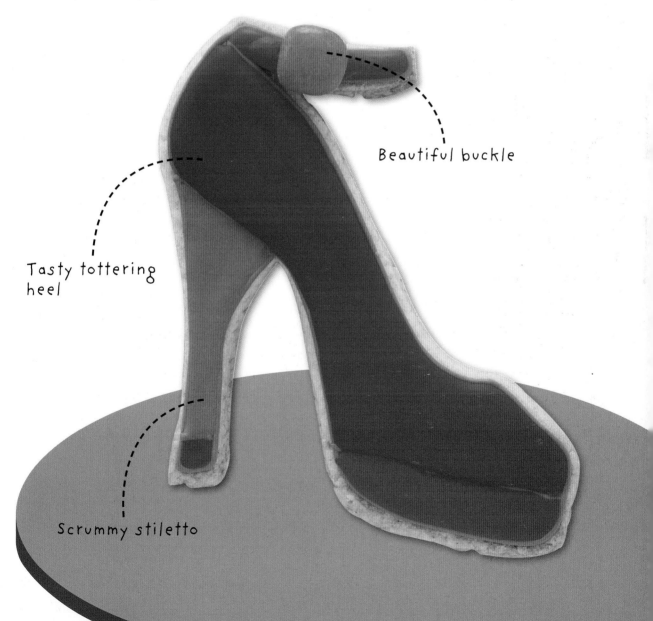

Beautiful buckle

Tasty tottering heel

Scrummy stiletto

Vintage Dress

Ingredients

- 1 quantity lemon cookie dough (see page 7)
- Flour, for dusting
- 1 quantity royal icing (see page 11)
- Lilac and green food coloring
- Lemon juice, for thinning
- 1³/₄ yards (1.5 metres) green ribbon, about 1-cm (¹/₂-inch) wide

Equipment

- Large cookie sheet
- Rolling pin
- Parchment, for tracing
- Pencil
- Scissors
- Small sharp knife
- 3 paper pastry bags (see page 17)
- Fine round decorating tip
- Toothpick

Baking: Heat the oven to 375°F (190°C, Gas 6). Grease a large cookie sheet, and trace and cut out the dress template on page 125. Roll out the dough on a lightly floured surface until about ¹/₄ inch (5 mm) thick, then cut around the template to shape 6 cookies. Place the dough shapes on the cookie sheet, spacing them slightly apart. Gather up the trimmings and reroll to make extra cookies, if liked. Bake in the preheated oven for 12–15 minutes until lightly browned around the edges. Remove from the oven, leave on the cookie sheet for 2 minutes, and then transfer to a cooling rack to cool completely.

Dresses: Put 2–3 tablespoons of the royal icing in a paper pastry bag fitted with a fine plain decorating tip. Use to pipe outlines around the edges of the cookies. Reserving 3 tablespoons of the remaining royal icing, add a little lilac food coloring and a few drops of lemon juice to the rest of the icing to give a thinner consistency (see page 19). Put the icing in a separate paper pastry bag and snip ¹/₄ inch (5 mm) off the tip. Pipe the icing inside the outlined areas of the dress, spreading it out with a toothpick. Leave to set for several hours or overnight.

Lace: Beat green food coloring into the remaining 3 tablespoons of royal icing, adding a little at a time until the desired shade is reached. Put in a pastry bag fitted with a fine round decorating tip and use to pipe squiggly lines and dots around the bases and sleeves of the dresses to represent lacy trim.

Ribbons: Cut the ribbon into lengths of about 9-inches (23-cm). Wrap the ribbon around the waists of the cookies and tie into bows.

Cookie-rella, you shall go to the ball

Delicate ribbon belt

Smooth royal icing

Luscious lace

Mask

Ingredients

- 1 quantity vanilla cookie dough (see page 6)
- Flour, for dusting
- $5^1/_2$ oz (150 g) pale gray rolled fondant
- Confectioners' sugar, for dusting
- 1 quantity vanilla buttercream (see page 10)
- Red and black food coloring
- 100 g ($3^1/_2$ oz) black rolled fondant
- $^1/_2$ quantity royal icing (see page 11)
- Pearlescent dragées
- 1.1 yards (1 meter) gray ribbon

Equipment

- Large cookie sheet
- Rolling pin
- 3-inch (7.5-cm) round cookie cutter
- Parchment paper
- Pencil
- Scissors
- Tray
- Small sharp knife
- Small spatula
- Paper pastry bag (see page 17)
- Fine round decorating tip

Baking: Heat the oven to 375°F (190°C, Gas 6) and grease a large cookie sheet. Roll out the dough on a lightly floured surface until about $^1/_4$ inch (5 mm) thick and cut out 6 cookies using a 3-inch (7.5-cm) round cookie cutter. Place the dough rounds on the cookie sheet, spacing them slightly apart. Gather up the trimmings and reroll to make extra cookies, if liked. Bake in the preheated oven for 12–15 minutes until lightly browned around the edges. Remove from the oven, leave on the cookie sheet for 2 minutes, and then transfer to a cooling rack to cool completely.

Masks: Trace and cut out the mask template (see opposite). Line a tray with baking parchment. Roll out the gray rolled fondant on a surface dusted with confectioners' sugar until about $^1/_{16}$ inch (2 mm) thick, and cut around the template. Repeat to give 6 masks. Transfer the masks to the paper-lined tray and leave for several hours or overnight until set.

Base: Beat deep red food coloring into the buttercream, adding a little at a time until the desired shade is reached. Spread the buttercream over the cookies using a spatula.

Cloak: Roll out the black rolled fondant until about $^1/_{16}$ inch (2 mm) thick, then cut out 6 shapes that are roughly triangular. You want the each side to measure about $2^1/_4$ inches (6 cm) each. Lay the cloaks over the cookies, folding them slightly.

Finishing touches: Color the royal icing with black food coloring until it is the same color as the masks. Put the icing in a paper pastry bag fitted with a fine round decorating tip and use to pipe a decorative edge around each of the masks and outline the eye holes. Press about 16 pearlescent dragées into the piping on each mask, spacing them evenly apart. Cut the ribbon into 6 pieces and fold roughly in half. Secure one piece to the back of each mask using a little icing from the pastry bag, then secure the masks to the cookies using more icing.

Pretty pearls

A most mysterious munch

Art Attack

Ingredients

- 1 quantity lemon cookie dough (see page 7)
- Flour, for dusting
- 1 quantity royal icing (see page 11)
- Lemon juice, for thinning
- Red, black, blue, and yellow food colorings

Equipment

- Large cookie sheet
- Rolling pin
- Small sharp knife
- Tray
- Baking parchment

Baking: Heat the oven to 375°F (190°C, Gas 6) and grease a large cookie sheet. Roll out the dough on a lightly floured surface until about $1/4$ inch (5 mm) thick and cut out six 4 x 2.5-inch (10 x 6.5-cm) rectangles. Place the dough shapes on the cookie sheet, spacing them slightly apart. Gather up the trimmings and reroll to make extra cookies, if liked. Bake in the preheated oven for 12–15 minutes until lightly browned around the edges. Remove from the oven, leave on the cookie sheet for 2 minutes, and then transfer to a cooling rack to cool completely.

Canvas: Beat the royal icing with enough lemon juice so that it levels smoothly when the spoon is lifted from the bowl. Spread the icing over the cookies, making sure that it covers the sides as well. Place on a cooling rack over a tray lined with parchment paper to catch the drips.

Paints: Divide the remaining royal icing into 4 small bowls or cups, and color each with one of the food colorings—red, black, blue, and yellow. Test the consistency of the icing on a piece of paper before decorating the cookies—it should be thin enough to drizzle in fine lines with a teaspoon. If necessary, thin again with a few drops of lemon juice. Using a teaspoon, drizzle lines of the different colored icings over the white icing on each cookie. Leave to set for several hours or overnight.

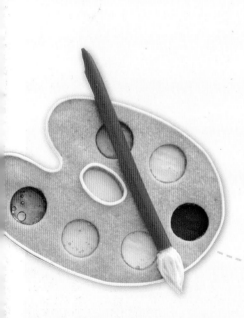

Try me too! page 48

SPLAT!
splash!

A masterpiece!

Go crazy with icing paint

see what else is beautifully patterned...

Ammonite Fossil

Ingredients

- 1 quantity vanilla cookie dough (see page 6)
- Flour, for dusting
- 2 quantities vanilla buttercream (see page 10)
- Pink and blue edible decorating dusts

Equipment

- Large cookie sheet
- Rolling pin
- Parchment paper, for tracing
- Pencil
- Scissors
- Small sharp knife
- Small spatula
- Fine paintbrush

Baking: Heat the oven to 375°F (190°C, Gas 6). Grease a large cookie sheet, and trace and cut out the ammonite fossil template on page 125. Roll out the dough on a lightly floured surface until about $1/4$ inch (5 mm) thick, then cut around the template to shape 6 cookies. Place the dough shapes on the cookie sheet, spacing them slightly apart. Gather up the trimmings and reroll to make extra cookies, if liked. Bake in the preheated oven for 12–15 minutes until lightly browned around the edges. Remove from the oven, leave on the cookie sheet for 2 minutes, and then transfer to a cooling rack to cool completely.

Fossil: Spread a thin layer of buttercream over the cookies using a small spatula. Once evenly covered, tilt the spatula at an angle and, working from the center of the fossil, use the tip to mark up grooves in the buttercream. Turn the cookie as you work to create the fossil pattern. Repeat for the remaining cookies.

Finishing touches: Dip a paintbrush in a little pink decorating dust and flick it around the edges of the cookies. Repeat with the blue dust.

Jurassic cookie

Fun fossil patterns

Sparkly sprinkles

Templates

38 / Festival Elephant

100 / Kiddie's Car

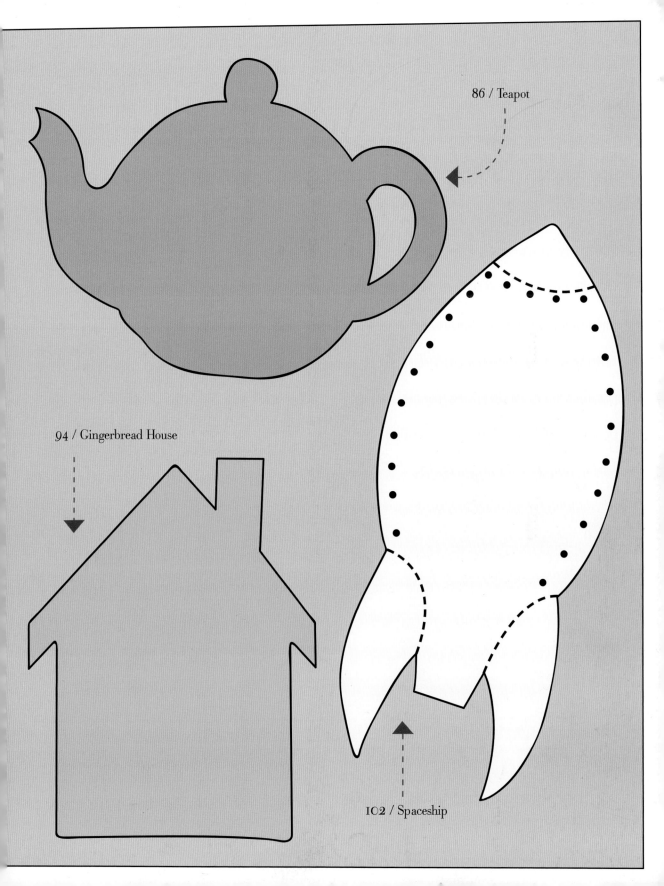

86 / Teapot

94 / Gingerbread House

102 / Spaceship

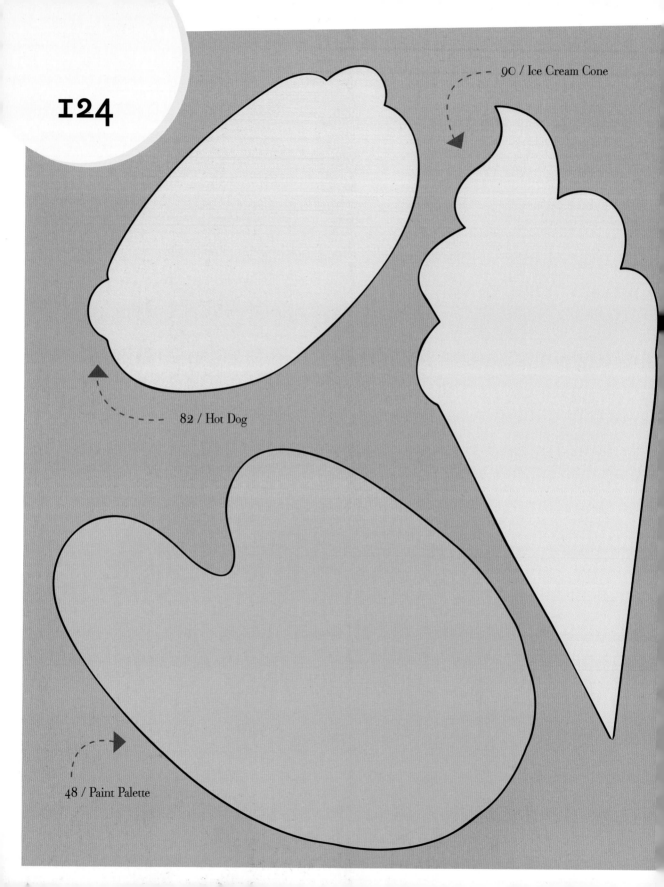

90 / Ice Cream Cone

82 / Hot Dog

48 / Paint Palette

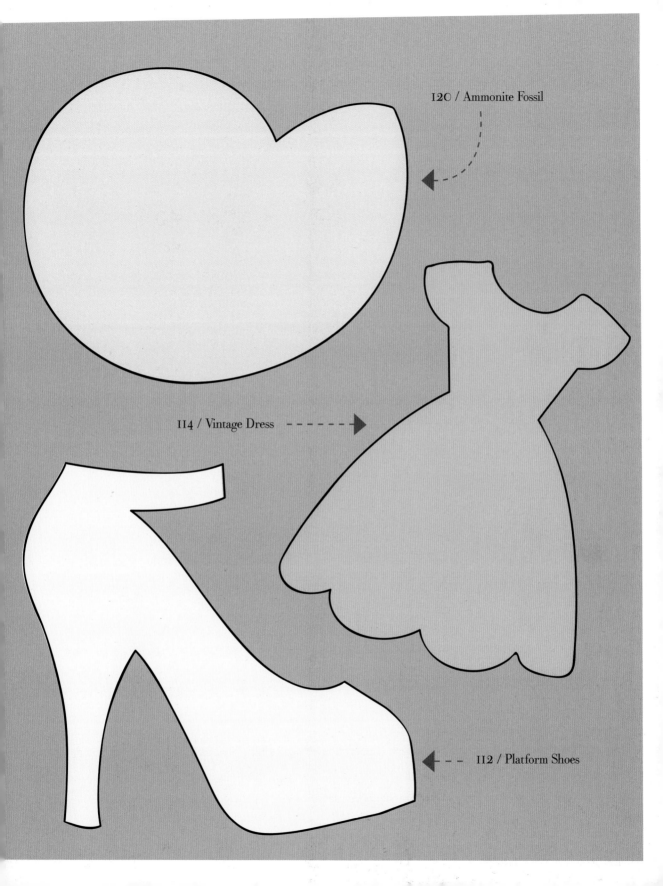

120 / Ammonite Fossil

114 / Vintage Dress

112 / Platform Shoes

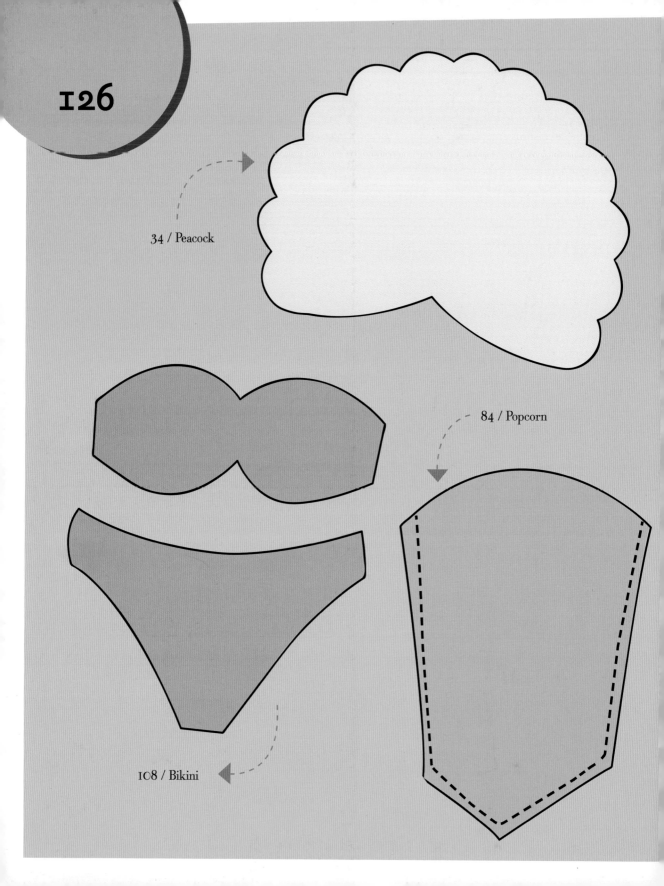

34 / Peacock

84 / Popcorn

108 / Bikini

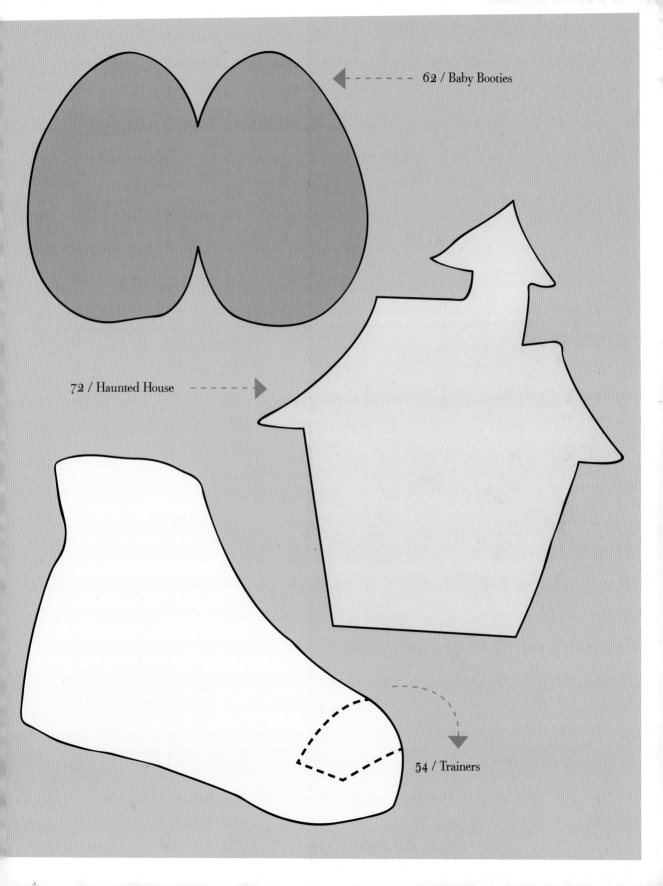

62 / Baby Booties

72 / Haunted House

54 / Trainers

Source List

Internet sources for decorating ingredients and sugarcraft equipment supplies. Many of the companies also have retail locations.

USA

A.C. Moore
Online and retail supplier
Tel. 1-800-ACMOORE
www.acmoore.com

Global Sugar Art
Online supplier
Tel. 1-800-420-6088
www.globalsugarart.com

Jo-Ann Fabric and
Craft Store
Online and retail supplier
Tel. 1-888-739-4120
www.joann.com

Michaels Stores, Inc.
Online and retail supplier
Tel. 1-800-MICHAELS
www.michaels.com

N.Y. Cake & Baking Dist.
Online supplier
56 West 22nd Street
NY, NY 10021
Tel. 212-675-CAKE
www.nycake.com

Pfeil & Holing
Online supplier
Tel. 1-800-247-7955
www.cakedeco.com

Wilton Homewares Store
Online and retail supplier
Tel. 1-800-794-5866
www.wilton.com

Canada

Creative Cutters
Online supplier
1-888-805-3444
www.creativecutters.com

Golda's Kitchen
Online supplier
Tel. 1-866-465-3299
www.goldaskitchen.com

Michaels Stores, Inc.
Online and retail supplier
Tel. 1-800-MICHAELS
www.michaels.com

UK

Almond Art
Online supplier
Unit 15/16, Faraday Close
Gorse Lane Industrial Estate
Clacton-on-Sea
Essex CO15 4TR
Tel. 01255 223 322
www.almondart.com

Blue Ribbon Sugarcraft Centre
Online and retail supplier
29 Walton Road
East Molesey
Surrey KT8 0DH
Tel. 020 8941 1591
www.blueribbons.co.uk

Jane Asher Party Cakes
Online and retail supplier
24 Cale Street
London SW3 3QU
Tel. 020 7584 6177
www.janeasher.com

Squires Kitchen Shop and
School
Online and retail supplier
Squires House
3 Waverley Lane
Farnham
Surrey GU9 8BB
Tel. 0845 22 55 671
www.squires-group.co.uk

Australia & New Zealand

Cake Deco
Online and retail supplier
Shop 7, Port Philip Arcade
232 Flinders Street
Melbourne, Victoria
Australia
Tel. 03 9654 5335
www.cakedeco.com.au

Milly's
Online and retail supplier
273 Ponsonby Road
Auckland
New Zealand
Tel. 0800 200 123
www.millyskitchen.co.nz

South Africa

Kadies Bakery Supplies
Online and retail supplier
Kingfisher Shopping Centre
Kingfisher Drive
Fourways
Gauteng
South Africa
Tel. 027 11 465-5572
www.kadies.co.za